BRAINERD
SHOP DOGS

BRAINERD SHOP DOGS

A HISTORY OF
NORTHERN PACIFIC RAILROAD WORKERS

BOB ROSCOE WITH CARLA ROSCOE

THE
History
PRESS

Published by The History Press
Charleston, SC
www.historypress.com

Opposite: Shop dogs in front of a wooden boxcar. Jim Roscoe is third row, second from left. *Photo courtesy of Crow Wing County Historical Society.*

First published 2023

Manufactured in the United States

ISBN 9781467150590

Library of Congress Control Number: 2023932120

In memory of my dad, Jim Roscoe, a blue-collar shop dog who worked at the Brainerd shops as his lifelong career, I dedicate this book. I also wish to collectively include his fellow shop dogs, whom he worked with sometimes shoulder to shoulder; my brother John, an accomplished writer with whom I shared authorship of a previous book; my brother Bill, who worked as a shop dog in summers between his college years and has significantly contributed to this book; and my sister, Mary, who shared family suppers as we listened to our dad's insightful observations of his railroad workday. My daughter, Carla, has provided immense editorial assistance, and my son, Neal, shared his insights during discussions concerning his grandfather's railroad work. I wish to thank my wife, Sally, who has provided me with inspiration for my writing efforts. These shop dog stories may at times lack actual facts, but a story can tell a truth in itself—and maybe in a better if not also more interesting way.

CONTENTS

CONTENTS

ACKNOWLEDGEMENTS

Our dad's suppertime observations are what instigated me, with the help of my brothers, John and Bill, and my sister, Mary, to write this book. My brother John has been a constant guide to my last several years of writing, as have other members of my Saint Cloud Writers Group: Marilyn Brinkman, Marcia Neely, Bill Morgan and Arlys Krim. I thank the Crow Wing County Historical Society, notably Hillary Swanson, Margaret O'Rourke and Brian Marsh. I especially thank my brother Bill Roscoe, who worked at the shops during three summers in the 1960s and knew most of the shop dogs described in this book. His input on their nicknames and exploits has been invaluable. He definitely qualifies as a shop dog.

INTRODUCTION

WHAT'S IN A NICKNAME?

Minnesota Public Radio's *Friday Morning Marketplace Report* on September 5, 2014, carried a feature called "Security Princess or Engineering Manager?" For many years, Silicon Valley companies in California have allowed employees to pick their own titles (though not their real titles) for business cards. Names such as "Ruby on Rails Rockstar," "Software Ninja" and "Data Wrangler" are examples.

Management consultant Keith Rollag said findings have revealed this practice "actually reduced people's feelings of job exhaustion and it reduced the stress they felt while they're on the job." Those employees felt empowered to redefine their jobs in ways that felt more meaningful.

However, this idea did not start in the twenty-first century in Silicon Valley. Our dad worked at the Northern Pacific Railroad Shops in Brainerd, Minnesota, in the railroad car fabrication building for over four decades of the twentieth century. In that building, almost all of the railroad laborers, boxcar assemblers, welders, supply keepers and others had nicknames with dubiously fanciful words.

A notable distinction was that these nicknames were not self-chosen but given to them by their fellow railroad workers. They were not meant to be complimentary. Nicknames such as Lord Wheelbarrow, Pansy Norquist, Corduroy Johnson, Chicago Pete and the Soo Line Bull are a few of the many. These men led very straightforward lives and conformed to every norm. But an unfortunate or awkward mistake could render a railroad worker a label he would live with for the rest of his life.

How Railroad Workers
Gained the Name "Shop Dogs"

In the northern Minnesota town of Brainerd, Northern Pacific railroad workers, with their very apt sense of ironic wit, collectively gave themselves the name "shop dogs." The name's origin is assumed to have given these men a perverse sense of honor, specifically to distinguish themselves in Brainerd's top-down social structure, most evident with the downtown business store owners' implicit and explicit deprecation at shop workers at that time. This railroad working culture was very adept at making their labor creatively maintained with healthy measures of back-and-forth satire in countless individual and unique circumstances. They developed well-practiced subtle as well as not-so-subtle wisecracks and verbal caricatures of each other.

Performing their labor sometimes nearly elbow to elbow perhaps provided the right opportunity for these workers to observe each other's singular traits up close, which included those mannerisms that could be crafted into comical situations, followed by opportunities to skillfully direct their ironic wisecracks aloud.

A job situation or social misstep could be deliberately misconstrued to the detriment of a hapless shop dog. In many instances, it was a personal trait, an unintended circumstance or the odd behavior of a shop dog that invited his fellow shop dogs to react to that predicament in a humorous way not easily forgotten.

The origin of the first utterance of the term *shop dog* is perhaps deservedly unknown. But its reference undoubtedly hit the mark at those not quite auspicious moments in a markedly class-conscious town.

In this northern Minnesota town of twelve thousand residents, both socioeconomic groups knew each other's status at all times. Throughout the 1940s into the 1980s, Brainerd contained two dominant although distinct social groups. The downtown businesses established themselves as the upper class of the city. They assumed they would be forever in control over the town's overall well-being.

Distinctly separate and of lower status, the blue-collar railroad workers performing manual labor unquestionably accepted their lower ranking. It should be emphasized that this manual labor supplied city retail stores and various businesses with substantial economic contributions from their railroad paychecks.

Shop dogs took pride in the hard work they performed and in receiving respect by fellow shop workers. The shop dog nickname purposely became a term of reverse snobbery, a recognition of identity that the railroad men could gain in their comfortable separateness from those of higher civic rank. The nickname formed shop dogs' solidarity of workers with whom they spent workday after workday in good times and hard times.

While not all shop dogs had nicknames, they shared stories and made them. Many stories had to do with human foibles. Some stories were about pranks on one another. There was a plenitude of stories about "carrying out" supplies or getting caught at it. Our brother John recalls,

> *In the summer, when I was home from college, my mother would ask me to drive over to the shops and pick up dad. Not long after the whistle blew, the workers began to pass through the gate. Dad was among the first group to appear. After he got into the car, he would encourage me to sit awhile, and he would point out, by name, many of the men still passing through the gate. In this way I was able to put a face to the many men he told stories about at home.*

These stories were undoubtedly shared and told in other shop dogs' families too, entering their own families' history and lore. There are undoubtedly shop dog stories unknown to this author, though it has been a family pursuit to remember and confirm with one another the shop tales heard over family suppers. "Who had the glass eye?" "How did Rudy Lindberg get away with his 'appropriations'?"

There are undoubtedly shop dog names that are not known to us, but we prompt one another to remember as many as we can and maintain a catalogue. "Who was Summer Kitchen?" "What was the shop dog's name who got the cement blocks put under the rear axle of his car?" Named and unnamed, the shop dogs built, welded, riveted and otherwise joined together a unique culture complete with lingo, humor and tales both tall and of regular height.

They built railroad boxcars, and they built railroad stories.

1

THE NORTHERN PACIFIC LAYS OUT A ROUTE THROUGH THE FUTURE TOWN OF BRAINERD

BRAINERD'S ORIGINS

The development of the Brainerd Northern Pacific Railroad shops was tied to Brainerd's own beginnings. In its initial stages, the Northern Pacific had planned to a build a bridge across the Mississippi River at Crow Wing, a settlement near the confluence of the Mississippi and Crow Wing Rivers. By the 1850s and '60s, Crow Wing had become a larger population center, roughly half of whom were Ojibwe. Crow Wing was at that time the northernmost settlement of European immigrants. And as in other regions in the upper Midwest and Canada, many fur trappers and traders in the area were Métis, which generally meant the children of Ojibwe women and men of European stock, mainly from France and the British Isles.

The railroad plan, however, was beset with difficulty. The trader and settler who owned much of the land at Crow Wing, Clement Beaulieu, demanded a high price from the Northern Pacific Railroad and proved intransigent in attempts at bargaining.[1]

The Northern Pacific then selected a different location. In 1870, construction crews were established on the east side of the Mississippi River to begin their layout work, near the present railroad bridge. They built a railroad bridge that soon provided the transportation of goods and supplies that strengthened both the Northern Pacific works and the growing town of Brainerd.

After the Northern Pacific completed rail service between Lake Superior and Brainerd, regular freight trains brought raw materials and other supplies into the burgeoning town and the railroad shops that were also increasing in importance. Passenger trains soon followed.

While Crow Wing had once been considered the county seat, Brainerd now attracted more of the region's commerce. By 1880, the population of Brainerd had grown to 1,865 and was officially designated the seat of Crow Wing County.[2]

THE NAMING OF BRAINERD

The land that became the town of Brainerd had been largely pine forest. With the lakes and river, it was a rich habitat for wildlife and for indigenous Ojibwe living there. The location had become known straightforwardly enough as the Crossing.

According to the *Brainerd Dispatch*, the name Brainerd was chosen in honor of the late Lawrence Brainerd, a U.S. senator, during a Northern Pacific board meeting. The president of the Northern Pacific had married the senator's accomplished daughter.

Whether this was indeed a direct honoring of the senator or an indirect honoring of his daughter, this family name was selected by the Northern Pacific in favor of Ogamagua, or Queen City. Ogamagua is from Ojibwe *ogimaakwe*, meaning female leader, boss, chief, queen.[3] This referred to the Ojibwe mother of the landowner and founder of Crow Wing, the same Clement Beaulieu who had asked the Northern Pacific an exorbitant price for the land.[4]

In 1870, the Northern Pacific Railroad began laying tracks. Plans and surveys for the rail bridge just outside Brainerd had been completed earlier that year; investor Jay Cooke and Company had put up $5 million to fund the enterprise. The basic footprint of the town now named Brainerd was planned out. Five hundred tons of iron had been shipped to Duluth and were waiting to be laid into track. What remained was grading along the projected path.

But after the basic plans for Brainerd had been finalized, claim jumpers converged on the area, staking claim on adjoining parcels of land. Like Clement Beaulieu, they too began to charge exorbitant asking prices for their land.

In response, the Northern Pacific loaded up its equipment and sent it by barge and horse team to Crow Wing, where it had originally surveyed and planned a crossing bridge. This maneuvering caused claim jumpers to lower their prices en masse, as described by local historian Carl Zappfe: "So fast as nearly to raise a wind." The railroad began to "snatch up Warranty and Quitclaim deeds off bargaining tables throughout the North Woods by the armful." The Northern Pacific then reloaded the barges and steamboats and wagons and brought their vehicles and supplies back upriver to Brainerd.[5]

The construction and trackage commenced. A trading post was established, followed by a boardinghouse, saloon and dance hall. The next year, the Northern Pacific built the Headquarters Hotel, a three-story edifice containing not only guest accommodations but also offices and other railroad-purposed rooms. Later in the year, the Northern Pacific established a depot and office building near the town center, where Brainerd's water tower, colloquially known as "Paul Bunyan's flashlight," now stands.[6]

The Northern Pacific was also formulating plans for a site including a machine shop, engine house and additional structures. By the following spring, the buildings were well underway. The first shop buildings were

A postcard of the passenger depot (now demolished). *Photo courtesy of Crow Wing County Historical Society.*

constructed almost a mile east of Brainerd's downtown area. They straddled the tracks, with most of the construction on the south side.

By April 1872, more than sixty tons of supplies and workings arrived to be formed into the machine shop. This new machine shop was declared the finest, as well as the largest, shop west of Albany, New York. At this point, there were only twenty-two locomotives on the entire line. They were all powered by wood-burning engines.[7] The Northern Pacific also invested in its own sawmill.

> *The Northern Pacific will build at once one of the largest saw mills in the country and cut their own lumber for the use of the entire road.... C.F. Kindred, president of the Brainerd waterpower company, verifies the announcement made exclusively in this paper on Tuesday, that the Northern Pacific company were going to build a mammoth saw mill at that place, and cut their own lumber. He says that the contract has been prepared and agreed upon and only awaits the signatures of the contracting parties to become final and binding. He also confirms the report that the Northern Pacific company have withdrawn their pine lands from the market.*[8]

The 1880s brought expansion of the Brainerd shops as well as Northern Pacific Railroad itself. The line originating in the Puget Sound on the northwest coast of California extended east into Montana. The Northern Pacific's line beginning at Lake Superior led west. The railroad famously and ceremoniously joined the two lines with a golden spike, forming the first transcontinental railway in the northern states.

Passenger transport between towns and relocating settlers became an increasing part of railroad business as the railroad expanded and prospered. Adding to the Northern Pacific's profits was the sale of land it had been granted as railroad right-of-way.

> *But it would do scant justice to the business acumen of the companies to say that they were interested in settlement merely as a means of selling their lands...railroad companies often found themselves with their lines completed, looking in vain for the traffic which would come only as the prairies were converted into homesteads. It came about, then, that the first great problem of these railroads was one of colonization.*[9]

Railroad workers in the 1880s. *Photo courtesy of Crow Wing County Historical Society.*

A worker measuring to make housing from a boxcar. *Minnesota Historical Society.*

Shipping wheat, cattle, lumber and various supplies for the burgeoning population and infrastructure of the area became part of the main business of the Northern Pacific Railroad.

The Northern Pacific also purchased ten blocks of land in the northeast part of the growing city for railroad workers to build homes. New residences for railroad workers' families began to spring up in the area near the railroad works, numbering somewhere from forty to sixty houses. These began to coalesce into the northeast neighborhood of Brainerd.[10]

2

THE NORTHERN PACIFIC RAILROAD SHOPS BUILDINGS

The Brainerd NP (Northern Pacific) shops were the most significant railroad facilities east of Livingston, Montana, and maintained most of the locomotives and freight rolling stock for the Northern Pacific, as well as over two thousand miles of trackage. They would be shifted or rebuilt during the late 1800s according to the expanding capacity of the railyard and the Northern Pacific main line and were rebuilt once due to fire.[11]

Local residents called the Northern Pacific by the initials "NP," and eventually came to refer to them as "the shops." Approximately twenty-five acres were required for the entire railyard site. It had its own fire department. The first layout of the Brainerd Northern Pacific Shops consisted of twenty-two industrial buildings occupying both sides of the east–west main line trackage.

Ten of these buildings still remain in the eastern portion of the railyard. The original car shops buildings were located on the north side of the main trackage. Constructed for locomotive and freight car repair, they could also fabricate new freight cars and locomotives. The materials yard was located on the west side of the car shops building, which facilitated bringing materials into the car shops.

The sloped roof-ridges in main shops buildings had built-in light monitors. They were structured by long iron beams and glazed side-wall panels. Thick brick walls and gabled roofs support these monitors, which add ample sunlight and ventilation for working spaces over twenty feet below. The sand-colored brick was supplied by the William Schwartz Brick Company located

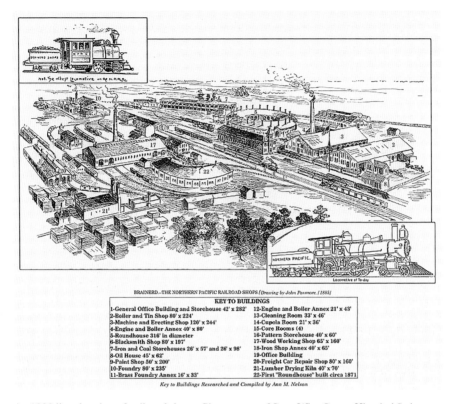

BRAINERD.—THE NORTHERN PACIFIC RAILROAD SHOPS [Drawing by John Passmore. [1885]

KEY TO BUILDINGS	
1-General Office Building and Storehouse 42' x 282'	12-Engine and Boiler Annex 21' x 43'
2-Boiler and Tin Shop 80' x 224'	13-Cleaning Room 33' x 46'
3-Machine and Erecting Shop 120' x 244'	14-Cupola Room 21' x 36'
4-Engine and Boiler Annex 40' x 80'	15-Core Rooms (4)
5-Roundhouse 316' in diameter	16-Pattern Storehouse 40' x 60'
6-Blacksmith Shop 80' x 197'	17-Wood Working Shop 65' x 160'
7-Iron and Coal Storehouses 26' x 57' and 26' x 98'	18-Iron Shop Annex 40' x 65'
8-Oil House 45' x 62'	19-Office Building
9-Paint Shop 50' x 200'	20-Freight Car Repair Shop 80' x 160'
10-Foundry 80' x 235'	21-Lumber Drying Kiln 40' x 70'
11-Brass Foundry Annex 16' x 33'	22-First "Roundhouse" built circa 1871

Key to Buildings Researched and Compiled by Ann M. Nelson

An 1888 line drawing of railroad shops. *Photo courtesy of Crow Wing County Historical Society.*

in northeast Brainerd. Other buildings included a boiler shop, tin shop, oil shop and machine shop. A blacksmith shop was built and later replaced with a larger building.

> *In June 1877 the NP shops consisted of the roundhouse, machine shop, car and carpenter shop, blacksmith shop, paint shop and foundry. One apparatus in the machine shop was a huge turning lathe able to turn two steel drive wheels at once. It was reported to be a magnificent piece of machinery and cost some $5,000; a hydraulic press used to press the wheels on and off the axles, capable of exerting a force of 120 tons, was also part of the machinery located there. A trip-hammer weighing 600 pounds, able to gently bend a piece of tin or smash dies to smithereens, was located in the blacksmith shop. The foundry produced molds for making car and engine wheels and contained molds and castings of everything needed on the railroad.*[12]

Miscellaneous smaller-sized buildings contained a paint shop, a foundry and brass foundry annex, woodworking shop and a lumber drying kiln. A major building was the wood-framed roundhouse; 316 feet in diameter, it had a 56-foot wrought-iron turntable at its center. The wood roundhouse was later replaced by a masonry-and-steel structure.

The sheer number of individual workshops not only point to the number of jobs the NP shops provided. It also meant that many people employed in them became skilled workers. Along with clerks and laborers, the shops employed workers in skilled trades: "The number of men at present employed in the Northern Pacific railroad shops was 503. They were classified as follows in the different departments: carpenters, 175; blacksmiths, 60; machinists, 92; boilermakers, 27; tinsmiths, 14; moulders, 19; round house men, 38; yard laborers, 28; office clerks, 13; painters, 38."[13]

The Brainerd shops trained workers in trades important to railroad operations. A laborer could become a tinsmith, for example. Because railroads had the means and the drive to expand, they used the emerging technology of the latter part of the nineteenth century on a grand scale. While there had been some electricians and master machinists at that time,

Workers outside a blacksmith shop. *Photo courtesy of Crow Wing County Historical Society.*

in the century to come, there would be an explosion in the need for workers skilled in these trades.

The new century brought new construction and improvements supporting such changing and expanding works. In 1910, W.J. Hoy Construction Company had been given the contract for significant expansion. A pattern shop and storehouse were built, as well as several warehouses, including those for raw coke and coal. A new foundry was also constructed, which would later produce over six hundred tons of cast metal per month.[14]

The NP would continue to build and adapt structures on the site when needed. The car shops where our dad worked were not constructed until much later. They were built on the north side of the tracks during the mid-'40s in an industrial modern architectural style. Its flat roof and red brick walls set it apart, although it was not architecturally disruptive, from the beige brick and sloped roofs of the 1870s main buildings built approximately sixty years before.

Ten buildings and two structures would eventually be listed in the National Register of Historic Places as a historic district.

STEAM-POWERED LOCOMOTIVES

Early steam locomotives moved only in forward direction. Previously, trains were made to reverse direction by means of a combination of detaching the engine, running the engine on adjacent tracks and hooking the engine up to either end of the train, sometimes referred to as the "run around" method.

The use of turntables made changes in direction much easier, and roundhouses were built to accommodate changing of track and direction. The turntables they housed were surrounded by platforms on which tracks had been laid in radial arrangement. Steel rollers beneath rotated them to align with the trackage on the platforms, enabling locomotives to move forward on tracks connecting to their rolling stock and leading to destinations within the railyard and beyond.[15]

Locomotives today are powered by diesel and can move forward or in reverse on tracks. Push-pull locomotives have powered cabs at both ends to move the locomotives in either direction.

The railroad's first roundhouse would be destroyed by fire. The next roundhouse built served well past the turn of the century. Roundhouses became obsolete by mid-century, and the Brainerd shops demolished theirs in 1950. Though the tracks were ripped out, the concrete between them remains to this day in what was described as "pie-shaped" during the process of historic designation in the National Register of Historic Places and was listed as part of the historic district.

A Large Shops Fire

By the spring of 1882, a foundry had been completed. The brick-walled foundry had an iron-truss roof. Forty moulders were employed in its construction. Moulders prepare cast forms into which molten metal is poured. Iron roof trusses for the machine and erecting shops were well underway.

Extensive construction continued. West of the nearly completed machine shops, a new boiler was built, as were tank and tin shops. These enormous buildings functioned together, containing a transfer table that moved along a sliding platform. The transfer table was used to move locomotives to tracks at the end of the platform. A main office and storehouse were built between the roundhouse and the main tracks. The front west elevation features a sixty-five-foot-high clock tower. This brick building with its iron-trussed slate roof remains today a handsome architectural signature for the entire site. Aside from its purpose as a main office for the superintendent, it was also used for offices of other administrative divisions.

Several shop buildings were destroyed in a large fire on March 28, 1886. Fire raged through the north area of the railyard. The machine shops as well as the wood-planing shop, pattern shops and a handful of smaller buildings were destroyed. They were all wood-framed structures built in the previous decade and had constituted the original shops.

The fire may have likely originated from sparks from the smoke stack which ignited a pile of shavings in the dust tower. Quite a breeze was stirring at the time, which, in a very few seconds fanned the flames into a disastrous fire. The buildings burned constituted the original plant of the railroad shops and were built in 1871. The main shops, which stand south of the track were put up in 1880, and are built of brick and stone with slate roofs. There are six of these large buildings which were not injured by the fire. It is confidently predicted that the company will at once erect larger buildings of a fireproof character to take the place of the burned ones, thus greatly increasing the capacity of the shops at this point. The disaster, it is understood, will not materially interfere with the orders now on hand, as the company has ample facilities for getting out the work. [16]

Also a victim of the fire was the original roundhouse. The newer brick buildings situated south of the main tracks escaped destruction. These six structures were the main shops at the time of the fire. The aftermath was inspected by Superintendent Cushing.

> *He is of opinion that larger and more substantial buildings entirely fireproof will be immediately erected upon the site of the burned shops, and railroad officials generally state that there is hardly a doubt but this will be done. The original policy of the railroad company concerning the plant here will be followed just as if there had been no fire. Mr. Cushing says the burned buildings were 14 years old, and had lasted a great deal longer than he expected them to when he built them. The company can now carry out the plans they have had in contemplation for several years, of replacing the old wooden buildings with larger buildings of brick and stone....Instead of any of the workmen being thrown out of employment by the fire, the full force went to work as usual this morning....It was stated that all the men at the shops aggregating 600, will be put on full time of 10 hours per day, within a few days, and that a still further increase of 25 men has been ordered and will be added before the week is over.[17]*

The Northern Pacific rebuilt the areas on the north side of the tracks beginning on May 1 of that year. The buildings were to replace the current shops and were finished ninety days from the start.

By the late 1880s, the shops built the majority of freight cars, and serviced most of the locomotives, for the entire Northern Pacific main line, as well as for several branch lines east of the Rocky Mountains.[18]

The railyard provided work for approximately eight hundred men. These workers not only powered the Northern Pacific's success, but their families contributed greatly to the growing city of Brainerd, whose population increased, commerce escalated and neighborhoods took root. Decisions for further building in the railyard contributed to economic stimulus and civic good will.

> *This action on the part of the company will greatly stimulate the construction of new buildings and make the next few years the best Brainerd has ever seen. The council did wisely when they so readily and unanimously took the action desired by the company, for the N.P. railroad always has been, and is to-day...Brainerd's best friend.[19]*

This symbiotic relationship between the Northern Pacific shops and the Brainerd area in general would strengthen in the coming years.

Boxcars and building, circa 1930. *Photo courtesy of Crow Wing County Historical Society.*

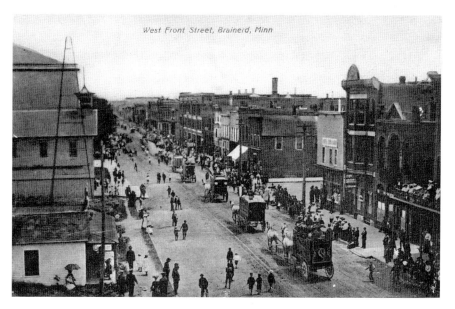

A postcard of West Front Street, Brainerd, Minnesota. *Photo courtesy of Crow Wing County Historical Society.*

THE POWER PLANT

A few decades later, a new power plant was being planned. This would be a large facility separate from the shops. In its distance and design, it would be safer from fire than the current power works that adjoined the wood-planing shop. The new larger power plant would be an expensive investment for the Brainerd shops. According to the *Brainerd Dispatch* (December 30, 1920), the improvements would include installation of mechanical stokers capable of burning coal dust.

Most of the inside is "overwhelmingly devoted to various engineering functions." The inner workings of this immense new power plant were also enormous. They needed to be, given the way they functioned: "A switch engine with hopper cars brings coal up an inclined ramp and dump the coal into two concrete hoppers with a capacity of 200 tons each. Below the concrete hoppers, coal passes to a shifting table, which supplies coal to a traveling conveyor that carries coal to the coal crusher."[20]

They were also designed for operator safety. The machines that fed coal to boilers could be stopped at a few different points. Workers would not have to physically work with coal, and coal ash in the basement was mitigated with water sprays, presumably greatly reducing workers inhaling the dust.

The ashes drop from the stoker grate into ash hoppers, located in the basement. These hoppers have doors in the bottom which are opened and closed by compressed air and ashes are dropped into cars located below the hoppers. There is a spray of water into the ash hopper which cools the ashes and keeps down dust. There is no handling of coal or ashes by manual labor in the plant.[21]

While designed to be functional, the power plant has been appreciated for its aesthetics. The Crow Wing County Historical Society's records include a wonderful description of the building's physical structure. "The power plant has an architectural composition of cube shapes with plain walls, large squarely shaped windows flanked each side by a pair of tall, slightly tapered smokestacks perhaps architecturally unintended, but evoking an industrial modernist elegance."[22] That these immense smokestacks were not constructed of concrete but of brick is an engineering marvel.

Here is one place that a true brick building lover will thoroughly enjoy. When you are driving into the old downtown of Brainerd, you will quickly

An aerial view of the roundhouse and power plant. *Photo courtesy of Crow Wing County Historical Society.*

spot some large smokestacks in the skyline. This tells you where the Northern Pacific shops are located. Although it does not appear that either of these smokestacks was made out of brick, they are quite tall.[23]

The power plant, slated for destruction in 1978, escaped the wrecking ball and would become part of the historic district listed in the National Register of Historic Places. Though boarded up, occasional trespassers explored. After one such exploration in the 1990s, my daughter began to refer to it as a cathedral of dead tech. The power plant was boarded and sealed more effectively during the last few decades.

3

BUILDING BOXCARS

Wood Boxcars

A new car shops building was planned toward the end of the Second World War. Shops operations increased greatly after its construction in 1945. Made of brick and steel, this building expanded the railyard's capacity enormously and had the biggest impact on the city of Brainerd since the first shops began operations in the previous century.

According to Brian Marsh, administrator of the Crow Wing County Historical Society, ground preparation for the car shops building began in 1944, but the construction of the building didn't start until the spring of 1945.

During the initial excavations, human bones were discovered:

> *Here is a small interesting item about preparing the ground for a new car shop building: When earth was removed from another area of the shops for use to fill, to everyone's surprise, the excavators started unearthing skeletons. The remains of seven people were later buried in Evergreen Cemetery and an Unknown Pioneers marker commemorates these very early residents of what became Brainerd.*[24]

The Brainerd car shops building is a modern style, a long rectangular flat roof structure with large doors on the east and west ends. The car shops building's modernist industrial architecture set it apart, although it was not visually disruptive with the 1870s-era gable-roofed traditional beige brick architecture of the buildings south of the main tracks.

Loading a gondola. *Photo courtesy of Crow Wing County Historical Society.*

Outside the building was a vast yard with stacks of railroad car components. Large forklift tractors brought smaller components inside the car shops building for assembly, spotting their locations according to linear layout assembly procedures.

Most of the clear span interior was devoted to the assembly of freight cars. Completed railroad cars built on several pairs of rails within the structure would be rolled out on various sets of steel tracks several times a day.

Railroad cars were built in numbers that gave a name to programs. For example, boxcars may have been built as a four-hundred-car program. Other railroad cars such as flatcars and gondolas had smaller program numbers.

My brother Bill described the boxcar programs:

> *My thinking is that the boxcar building programs were somewhat competitive, especially in the '50s and '60s and that the Brainerd shops [were] noted for its quality work building wooden boxcars on steel underframes. At one point they were rolling out eight cars a day. I know that there was some competition from contractors of NP in the later years. I think that [the] boxcar building at the Brainerd shops became phased out because the steel cars had a much longer functional life compared to the wooden cars. I would assume that railroad freight cars built in the '50s and '60s are still rolling.*

Older boxcars used wood construction for wall framing, occasionally using diagonal surface-applied structural reinforcement. The siding material was high-quality vertical fir members approximately a full inch thick and five inches wide, nail-fastened to backup framing. The vertical face of one side end had a "tongue" (a thin strip set outward) and fit into the "groove" (a slot cut into one end that joined the tongue of an adjoining member). The tongue-and-groove (called "T and G") provided more strength and weather-tight protection than a series of flat wooden boards. Sliding doors on boxcar sides guided by top and bottom guide strips provided access for loading and unloading freight, some with bulky sizes, located on both sides of the boxcars. Sheet metal with specialized shapes was attached in strategic material joinery for weather protection.

These wood boxcar bodies were probably "stick-built"—in very small assemblies, mostly one or a few wood members at a time—with hand carpentry labor assisted by basic platforms and ladders. Surfaces were initially hand painted but later spray finished when industrial spray paint devices were made available.

Wood boxcars being assembled. *Minnesota Historical Society.*

Freight cars were painted "Tuscan red"—basically a slightly dull maroon color, with the large, round Northern Pacific logo painted in black, red and white. The later-built Burlington Northern (BN) boxcars were "Cascade green." White letters and numbering were used in various areas of the boxcar face. This enabled individual identification of the boxcar and its routing throughout the nation's entire railroad track system. It is common for many boxcars to be connected to other railroad companies to deliver its contents to intended destinations throughout the nation.

According to my brother Bill, who worked at the shops for several summers, boxcars built in the Brainerd shops could be identified by an oval stencil on the frame of the car directly under the opening for the door: "Built in Brainerd, Minnesota" or "Built by the NPRR (Northern Pacific Rail Road) in Brainerd, MN."

One of the popular TV shows in the '60s was *The Fugitive*. It was about a doctor (Richard Kimball) who was mistakenly convicted of killing his wife and escaped while being transferred to prison. He maintained that a one-armed man actually killed her, and the show centered on him traveling the country looking for the one-armed culprit, who was always one step ahead of the police. In one episode, the police were closing in, and he hopped on a boxcar with the "Built in Brainerd MN" mark; the Brainerd railroad workers talked about that episode for weeks afterward.

BUILDING STEEL BOXCARS

Boxcars also needed protection from thieves. Enclosed boxcars and locking latches were the result. While wood boxcars were built start to finish at the place of fabrication, steel boxcars were fabricated with basic components made elsewhere and transported for expeditious assembly at the Brainerd shops. By mid-century, boxcar construction was transitioning from basic "stick-built" wood construction to all-steel design.

With the phasing out of wooden boxcars, the shops began to construct sturdier steel cars. They were stronger, lighter and cheaper. They could transport greater amounts of freight with less fuel.

Heavier machinery—and more welders, such as our dad—were needed to assemble them. Steel boxcar construction used an overhead. This huge machine lifted large sections of the top or "cap" into position. This stabilized the frame of the boxcar. The car under construction could be moved either way on rails built into the floor. Wheels and "trucks," the

Opposite, top: Building railroad car underframes. *Minnesota Historical Society.*

Opposite, bottom: A boxcar being assembled with traveling crane. *Minnesota Historical Society.*

Above: A wooden reefer boxcar. *Minnesota Historical Society.*

undercarriages of boxcars, were assembled on tracks perpendicular to the overhead crane.

The shorter end panels of the boxcar were fixed into position before the longer sides. Large steel sheets were welded together. Forklifts brought other sections and were occasionally used to "spot" them in place. Smaller forklifts assisted in the process. Further steps in parts assembly would finish the boxcar. A small diesel engine moved newly completed cars out to a track spur to await their destined purpose.

Other types of railroad cars were built in the car shops. A gondola has a low-wall box with an open top and can carry loose aggregate or various parts needing no weather protection. Flat cars consist of a basic platform on wheel assemblies with no sides or top and are used to transport vehicles and large equipment and containers, typically strapped to the platform. Refrigerated boxcars (called reefers) were not built at the Brainerd shops; although the NP and other railroad systems did use them, they sourced them from another boxcar fabricator in their rolling stock.

Locomotives carry enormous weight and momentum. This necessitates power braking, as well as air pressure systems, for every car. When these brake systems were connected to the engine, an entire system of brakes was in operation. In 1968, an air brake shop was added to service air brakes for the cars. A wheel shop was also built to maintain freight car wheels for the railroad operation.

RIVET WORK

At first, acetylene welding was the typical welding method, but by the middle of the twentieth century, the shops had largely converted to electric arc welding. Later, rivets became widely used. These simple devices consist of a solid shaft with a head on one end; once installed, the headless end of a solid rivet is deformed and enlarged with a hammer or rivet gun to hold it in place and provide a solid connection. For many years rivets were widely used and riveter workers were skilled craftsmen. Electric welding has increasingly displaced riveting as a method for connection of structural members and metal sheets.

DISMANTLING AND "CUTTING DOWN"

In the late 1930s and early 1940s, the Brainerd shops received wooden freight cars from all over the NP system and stripped them down, as they were being replaced by the new steel cars built by the shops. My brother Bill commented that employees were told they could purchase lumber from the wooden cars, which began the efforts for railroad workers to use the lumber to build their homes, additions to their existing homes and garages. The backyards of shop workers' houses had stacks of lumber ready for use in our railroad worker neighborhood. The railroad continued this dismantling until all-steel boxcars were well into fabrication.

Bill remembers, "My work consisted of dismantling the trucks, wheel assemblies of boxcars that were being torn apart for salvage. At that time, the railroad was still transitioning from wooden cars to steel cars. I also spent some time removing various materials for the dismantled cars, mainly decking."

Many engines were taken to the Brainerd shops for "cutting down" during the 1950s. Welders like our dad used cutting torches for the monumental task

A partial view of the shop yard. *Minnesota Historical Society.*

of cutting down engines and steel boxcars. One such instance was cutting down the Number 5000. The Northern Pacific Railroad had acquired the world's largest steam engine. Constructed in 1928, it was called Number 5000 and served the Livingston, Montana area.

When Number 5000 needed substantial repair, the cost to overhaul it was prohibitively enormous. In 1952, the Northern Pacific sent it to the Brainerd shops to be disassembled. What couldn't be salvaged outright would be scrapped and remelted. According to the *Brainerd Dispatch*,

> *The locomotive and its tender attached behind for storing coal and water weighed 412 tons, measured over 85 feet long and burned 25 tons of coal every 50 miles. Engine and tender together were a total length of 130 feet. The coal was fed from tender to fire box with a screw type mechanical feeder. The tremendous cost of an overhaul job would not prove worthwhile. As a result, the shops consigned the 5000 to a "cutting down" process. In 1952 the mighty machine was dis-assembled by cutting torches and wrenches.*

4

HOW OUR PARENTS
CAME TO BRAINERD

Much like most people in rural pre–World War II Minnesota, our parents began their lives growing up in a rural area near various family members. Both of my parents had formed their early lives in the predominately agricultural area in Platte Lake Township in the southeastern part of Crow Wing County. Both were raised on farms with often precarious economics in that area.

They followed the local migratory pattern of many of the rural people around them, when the significant limitations of farm life were being answered by emerging opportunities for men and women in the growing diversified economy of nearby towns in the late 1930s.

My mother, Eleanore Schley, grew up on the family farm, one of two sisters allowed to attend Normal School. This was a high school–level school that trained its pupils to become teachers themselves. Becoming a nurse, teacher or nun were the three main options young, unmarried women had in order to move beyond—or leave behind—the hardships of farm life.

My mother and her sister, my aunt Margaret, became teachers at small schools in the area. Later, my mother would describe the compensation she received as a teacher of a one-room schoolhouse. Her pay per month was the same amount a hired man and a horse would cost on a farm.

It's difficult not to consider, and reword, a more modern phrase—this was equal pay for comparable worth. This equation sounds backward, rural, sexist. But modern minds and expectations can scarcely appreciate the value of a farmworker, or a horse, during those days. It's also important to remember that my parents, born in the mid-1910s, grew up and began their adult lives during the Great Depression. Having a job at all was often the result of luck and hard work.

Our dad, Jim Roscoe, like others in his family, also worked at other family farms or wherever there was work. This was dependent on circumstantial and seasonal conditions. Young men in the previous century traveled from farm to farm for work if they had no other prospects. In these ways, the nineteenth century still held sway in rural unmodernized America during the Great Depression. Manpower, horsepower.

But after the Rural Electrification Administration began in 1935, many work projects came into being that provided jobs establishing electric service to farms and other locales in rural Minnesota.[25] Our dad worked for at least one of these programs. Another New Deal program was the Public Works Administration (PWA), which also provided many jobs. Our dad's employment in the PWA came to an immediate halt when he received news of a job at the NP shops while digging a sewer trench, a celebrated family story.

Increasingly, younger people began to build their lives away from farms as they moved to nearby small towns to develop skills for industrial tasks or to be store clerks. This was the usual choice for the young men of the area. Young women could train to become nurses or, like our mother, elementary school teachers.

Many of these people, including our parents, moved to Brainerd to settle into what became close neighborhoods where former farm families could live nearby each other and could structure familiarity into their transforming lives. These neighborhoods also gathered retired farmers from rural areas, which continued the lifelong connections of people who knew each other back in their townships.

Some railroad shop workers, accustomed to their rural roots, built houses in various places throughout Crow Wing County, within a half-hour drive to work. Living in town was not for their sense of life. Some of them eventually acquired a few farm animals and chickens and planted small plots of vegetables for home use.

NEIGHBORS KNEW EVERYONE'S FAMILY, BASIC HISTORY, RELIGION AND A FEW OR MORE PERSONAL MATTERS

Around our house at 916 South Twelfth Street, many of the neighborhood men worked at the shops. Until the early 1950s, almost all wives were homemakers, except those who were teachers or nurses. Our dad's welding foreman Lawrence Bourassa and his family lived across the street. Swanny (Carl) Erickson, a machinist, and his family lived across the alley. Swanny worked in the machine shop and employed his astute wit that gave us the rundown on the shop dogs he worked with. Nearby was the Walt Deming household. Hjelmer Erickson, a clerk in the storeroom, and his wife, Pearl, lived a half block away.

Some evenings after supper, our dad would sit in one of his hand-built wood lawn chairs in the front yard under the box elder trees, and soon Lawrence Bourassa and a few nearby shop dogs would join them, sometimes bringing a few long neck bottles of beer. The conversation usually centered on several things that happened during the day's work at the shops. Sometimes, a few shop dog wives came with their husbands but joined our mother in the kitchen, where coffee and family news sharing took place.

ETHNIC ORIGINS

The shop dogs' ethnic backgrounds typically had immigrant origins. Their families before them had come from northern and eastern European countries, many of them from Germany or Poland and many from Scandinavia.

Compared to the more conformist Swedish and Norwegian immigrants, Finnish people seemed to hold on to their cultural identity for a longer time. Their identity, like their language, was different. Many of them lived in southeast Brainerd in a particular area where their houses were very close to each other.

At that time, they were often referred to as "Finlanders" and were occasionally the subject of jokes about being backward, ironically also told by the Polish, themselves the popular subjects of "Polock" jokes. Finns were also known for working some of the hardest railroad tasks, such as laying tracks. Our dad admiringly remarked, "They sure could turn a wheel."

In midwestern towns, it was not uncommon to hear German, Norwegian, Polish and other languages of origin, especially from older people. Many people could speak or at least understand German. During my teenage years working at the National T grocery store, an old Polish farmer told me what my last name meant in Polish.

JIM ROSCOE BECOMES A SHOP DOG

Our dad worked in the car shops building with approximately four hundred workers assembling boxcars and other freight cars. His father, Joe, worked for many years in the machine shop, and his older brothers, Joe ("Dode") and Lawrence, worked there as well. Our dad started as a laborer, moving into skilled jobs as he gained working proficiencies, and had been working as a welder in railroad car fabrication for many years by the time he retired thirty-seven years later.

Our dad's job at the shops put his physical and mental skills to the best use available during this time in this small northern Minnesota town. His first day at the railroad in 1940 was preceded by the last day of his working at his temporary Public Works Administration (PWA) job. His workday came to an end after a literal lift-up from digging ditches for water and sewer lines in southeast Brainerd, as the town was developing its rudimentary public utilities. Working in a deep and muddy clay trench, moving his feet in his heavy boots was difficult in the dense clay. The incessant rain made the work deplorable, but it was the only way he could earn money for his new family, which now included me, the one-year-old Bob, their first child. While struggling in the muddy ditch with his shovel work, up on the street, he heard his shop dog brother Lawrence call down to him, "Jim, my foreman says you can start work at the shops tomorrow."

Our dad swung the blade of his shovel upward and held his hands tight near the top end of its long wood handle. Lawrence pulled on the knurled top of the shovel's metal blade. Putting one hand over the other and placing his feet, now out of his boots, against the side of the trench, our dad climbed up as Lawrence pulled in the shovel blade until our dad was standing on the ground. Lawrence told him to call down to the workers to pull his boots out of the mud and throw them up to him. Our dad told him, "Let the next poor sonofabitch to work down there have them."

Our dad's initial job at the shops was sweeping floors, a necessary task, but not a skilled or specialized one. He would soon become a laborer. Later he would gain skills, join the carman's union and train to become a carman welder. His long career was ahead of him.

After a year working at the NP shops, our dad applied at a savings and loan in downtown Brainerd. Working at the shops meant a secure job with decent pay. He received a loan, which was sort of a ten-year mortgage, with a monthly payment just under ten dollars. With this substantial start, he bought a nondescript lot 50 feet wide by 140 feet long at 916 South Twelfth Street on which he would build the family house.

This shop dog could soon begin the long process, filled with stories, of constructing his own house.

5

SHOP DOG HOUSES

In the late 1930s and early 1940s, the Brainerd shops were receiving wooden freight cars from all over the NP system, stripping them down, as they were being replaced by the new steel cars that the shops were building. Workers often purchased this salvaged lumber to augment new framing materials for the construction of their houses.

In addition, the NP regularly sold boxcars to people who fashioned them into lake cabins and as storage for various small-scale businesses in isolated parts of the city. One of these boxcars occupied the alley end of the lot near our house. Boxcar framing parts were likewise sold for their lumber for a variety of uses to workers for miscellaneous repairs. Our brother Bill remarked, "Most shop dogs lived in the lower-income parts of town with wood-frame houses that required frequent maintenance. A lot of shop dog time was spent talking about the work that their houses needed that the railroad would unknowingly furnish to keep their houses going."

The difficult Depression times still affected many northern Minnesota areas into the early 1940s. That sometimes meant the boxcar house was the only affordable roof over their heads. A small number of shop dogs fashioned their dwelling places out of one or more wood boxcars they could buy from the NP at a very low price. The shop dogs who bought boxcars to live in often called them "ramblers," because they rambled all over the country before they were brought back to the shops for salvage.

After their wheel assemblies and miscellaneous appurtenances were removed at the shops, a local house mover would use a special heavy-duty

Above: A shop dog converting a boxcar into a house in shops. *Minnesota Historical Society.*

Opposite: A handwritten note describing the boxcar-house conversion process. *Minnesota Historical Society.*

N.P.R.R. Shop. - Brainerd
C. A. Stanley, carman, screws hinges on front door to boxcar home. This first room will be combination kitchen, dining and living room. Cars are blocked up on the boxcar trucks to move thru shop on assembly line.

trailer rig that fit the boxcars on a pair of long, heavy beams to transport them to the site. Many shop dogs (although not all) removed the large sliding freight doors and framed the openings with a typical residential door. After installing windows, a low-pitched gabled roof to shed rain and often, but not always, rudimentary siding, it was minimally proper enough to receive relatives and company.

Two boxcars might be aligned alongside each other in a configuration that made a workable floor plan with two bedrooms and common living areas. Many railroad workers started with a small living place with two bedrooms if they had one or two children. If more children were born, this typically meant adding a conventional wood-framed addition as a lean-to on the original boxcar assembly. In the pretelevision era, some men built a large garage, out-building or remodeled a boxcar and started a side business such as welding, carpentry or machine repair.

These boxcar dwellings attempted to resemble typical houses, although many had telltale traces of their origins. Throughout the years, a porch might have been added, as well as a nearby garage and typical yard arrangements. Sometimes, when our family was driving in residential areas near the shops, our dad would point to a particular house and say, "A shop dog lives there."

Houses built from entire boxcars mostly appeared in the working-class areas of the town—northeast and southeast Brainerd—and their rudimentary appearances were accepted in their early days. The city was growing and their physical appearances were not seriously questioned. As Brainerd's citizens strived for higher living standards, the boxcar houses received increasingly more conventional exterior treatments to fit in with nearby houses.

Those boxcar domiciles with unconventional appearances eventually led Brainerd's citizens to grow less tolerant of these houses with unorthodox boxcar elements. At some point in time, as city government gained more organization, the Brainerd City Council revised the city's building codes to restrict whole shells of boxcars from becoming new dwellings.

Note: The previous description of railroad workers building their own houses with lumber they used from the shops, in the observation of this writer, might invite historic district designation of shop worker housing at some time in the near future.

JIM ROSCOE BUILDS THE FAMILY HOUSE IN SOUTHEAST BRAINERD

Many railroad workers, including our dad, built their houses with boxcar parts, such as wood beams for main structural support, interior wood framing from a local lumber yard and scrap boxcar siding for exterior wall sheathing. Wood components were fastened into place with nails transported out of the shops in lunch pails. They used various tools to build their houses that bore the imprint "NP."

In the 1950s, streets in this part of southeast Brainerd were unpaved. The dense clay underground was difficult and expensive to dig for a new basement. Accordingly, our dad decided to build a concrete foundation a few feet deep that would provide a main floor height just under three feet above grade.

Dad and my uncles Dode and Lawrence dug out the earth with long-handled number two shovels under the floor to a typical basement depth, poured a concrete floor and built concrete basement walls. The floor framing and subfloor material came from scrap dock lumber purchased at the shops. Lawrence and Dode also provided carpentry help to frame the first floor, walls and roof.

Our parents rented a tiny house a few blocks away during their new house construction work, placing a crib in a corner where I slept. They took in a drunken window maker in exchange for new windows for their house now under construction. They installed a space heater in the living room of their new house that provided basic warmth, and the other rooms were shut off with old blankets as needed. When the new house was weather-tight enough with new plaster walls and ceilings in the main living spaces and bathroom, our starter family moved in. A rudimentary kerosene-powered kitchen stove made meals possible, a space heater was located in the living room and kitchen cabinets were installed later. Soon my brother John was born and a small bedroom was readied for both of us to share a bed.

Seven years after starting construction, a furnace and ductwork were installed in the basement, and the house was basically finished. Wood siding and trim, with hardwood floors and basic kitchen appliances were substantial additions. By this time, our younger brother, Bill, was born, followed by our sister, Mary, completing the Roscoe family. Our dad built a rear bedroom addition for us three boys, and Mary took over the small bedroom in the original part of the house. Much later, a small closed-in front porch accommodated a sofa with a fold-out bed, useful when as adults, the four of us brought home our families for a weekend.

Most of the other houses in the area were one story with no front porches, typically clad with wood lap type siding and simple modest trim. Every window was double-hung type. Necessity allowed these houses to be absent of ornament, lending a composition where order dominates without being apparent and without the term "architecture" in consideration. The elements of proportion, balance or the attribute of beauty here find no importance. Neither is the balance between contrasting elements.

For the sake of applying the historians' insistence on architectural style, the term *vernacular* here is very much appropriate. Vernacular architecture is defined as a building type having no recognized style reflecting local traditions. At least originally, vernacular architecture did not involve architects but relied on the design skills and tradition of local builders. Our dad drew a simple floor plan with a carpenter's pencil on a shoebox cover. Further inquiry can reveal these southeast Brainerd houses as fitting what historical residential architecture books might define as "Minimalist Modern."

6

LIFE IN SOUTHEAST BRAINERD

RAILROAD WORKERS ALONG MY PAPER ROUTE

For several years I delivered the *Brainerd Dispatch*, along Route 9A, to over seventy houses in southeast Brainerd where I lived. Many were railroad shop dog homes. When it came to collecting the weekly payment, I learned how to deal with certain shop dogs. For instance, collecting from Arling Storstad on railroad payday evening was out of the question—Arling and his wife would be in the bars. The next night was my best chance. Arling would be home and happy to pay my bill. The following night was maybe OK. But after that, his paycheck was spent—or drunk up.

Fred Blocker and his wife, Mabel, were the opposite. On early payday night I'd knock on their back door (there were no doorbells yet in this era). Through the back-door window I'd see a hand reach up to the kitchen window sash and take away last week's receipt ticket. With a smile, Fred would open the door and hand me last week's receipt and a quarter and nickel. I would hand him the current receipt, which he'd dutifully place up on the window sash. After a short, "Hi, how are you?" I'd be on my way. A few customers later, I'd see Fred and Mabel's car back down their driveway—they waited for their paper delivery boy before they would head out for their favorite bar.

THE BOO GANG

A neighborhood family of Finns who lived on nearby Pine Street had a sister and three brothers. The brothers as little kids had become known by their neighbors as constant troublemakers who were always trying to start fights with other neighborhood kids but were not able to follow through. They gained the dubious nickname "Boo Gang," as they were unable to do more than actually scare anyone. "Boo" has a similar ironic meaning in Finnish.

As adults, the brothers' work at the shops came to an early end due to lack of self-discipline and showing up for work drunk in the morning.

When Pearl Harbor was attacked, beginning World War II, the Boo Gang aligned in formation on Pine Street, marched down to city hall and enlisted in the army. The *Brainerd Dispatch* proudly printed their photo on the front page. The *Dispatch* journalists intended to honor their patriotism, but their southeast neighbors joked that the nation would surely lose the war with the Boo Gang in the front lines.

All three brothers fought in combat and all of them returned to Brainerd after the war. They now expected due respect from people in Brainerd. But they soon returned to their drinking ways and remained known as the Boo Gang, often seen staggering drunk around downtown Brainerd and Little Hollywood.

SHOP DOGS' SONS AND SANDLOT BASEBALL

Our southeast Brainerd neighborhood was less than a mile from city limits. Vacant lots were common. Immediately south of our house was a pair of vacant lots. On one of them, a boxcar removed of its wheels rested on several concrete blocks, like other boxcars throughout southeast Brainerd. A storage boxcar owned by an appliance dealer was located against the alley, forming just the right backstop. My brothers and I and several other neighborhood boys became very interested in playing sandlot baseball. The pair of flat and tree-free lots provided just enough space as a baseball field for several years.

As we got older, stronger, with more skill, too many balls began to bang against the houses across street, somehow not breaking windows. Neighborhood dads promptly saw the need for another location. A few blocks farther south were other lots of vacant land, but with tall grass. Somebody knew the city crew who mowed city-owned land, and beer was made available. But a backstop was necessary. Unknown to Northern Pacific Railroad Shops management, several tall steel poles and sufficient wire mesh were installed by our dads. The city mowing crew continued to cut the grass, provided with liquid encouragement.

THE SHOPS WHISTLE

A steam-powered whistle at the power plant signaled the cardinal times of the workday and was loud enough to be heard all over Brainerd: 6:00 a.m. to awaken the shop workers, 7:00 a.m. when the workday started, 12:00 p.m. to announce lunch hour, 1:00 p.m. to resume work and 4:00 p.m. when the workday ended. In a symbolic way, the shop whistle asserted the railroad shop's highly significant role at that time in the economy and life of Brainerd. "Our daily schedules and rhythms were related to the shops," our sister, Mary, remembers.

Our dad would nearly be up out of bed by the time the six o'clock whistle stopped blowing. At seven o'clock, he was ready to begin his workday in the car shops. Saint Francis Catholic Church synchronized with railroad workers' lives by holding the first Sunday morning mass at seven o'clock, which our family attended. Other whistle times were very intermittent.

If night watchmen saw a fire in one of the buildings, the whistle would sound a series of long and short blasts. The pattern essentially telegraphed the location of the fire in the large shops yard. When the whistle sounded at night, the shop's fire department crew, made up from workers in various departments, would respond immediately, leaving their homes and rushing to the scene. Our dad was on this crew. When the night whistle blew, our dad would be awake quickly, getting ready to rush off to the fire. It was my job to help remember the sequence of long and short whistles.

Whistle blasts for nighttime derailments along the rail tracks led the derailment crews for sometimes long distances outside Brainerd. The crew would head out to clear the derailment wreckage and pull dislocated railroad cars back on the tracks with a crane mounted on a flat car. Sometimes, this took more than one day, but tracks were repaired as soon as possible so freight and passenger trains could resume operations. A damaged railbed could cause a series of freight cars or a locomotive to veer off the tracks.

JIM ROSCOE AND THE CITY COUNCIL

Our dad occasionally attended Brainerd city council meetings, out of his civic interests. He wanted to be generally informed about his part of town, especially concerning Southeast Twelfth Street, where we lived in the house he built in the early 1940s.

Perhaps the council spurred our dad's frustrations about how they conducted their business in relation to citizens of southeast Brainerd. He sensed, probably correctly, the council members didn't appreciate how he approached them, which was not how a shop dog should address those who socially and economically outranked him. At a particular council meeting, he commented about planned upgrades for Southeast Twelfth Street. For the most part the dirt street would be paved, and the open drainage ditch along street property lines would become enclosed in a metal culvert and covered with soil and turf.

Except in front of our house—the dirt street would remain along our block with the open drainage ditch. Our dad, equipped with a fifth-grade education, instinctively recognized what happens to the ranks of the working class when they confront city administration. They are "put in their place." But our dad persisted. Three years later, the paved street and covered metal culverts were finally installed in the block on which we lived, due to some process unknown to us.

7

SHOP DOG NICKNAMES

Karl Marx famously wrote, "From each according to his abilities, to each according to his needs." The NP shops did not operate by Marxist principles, but by fortunate circumstances, the disparate industrial tasks seemed to fit the spectrum of intelligence of their workers. Most often muscular effort was more needed than "head work."

Machinists and electricians were probably the smartest workers. Sweepers and common laborers who possessed minimal mental equipment fulfilled the most ordinary but necessary work. Pay scales were generally commensurate with ability. Providently, their wages, bolstered by unions, were decent enough to settle at the lower margins of the middle class. With the demise of railroad operations at the shops, Brainerd became less economically comfortable and, in its own way, less culturally enriched for its citizens at that time.

Along with their labor, the shop dogs curated a particular working-class culture. This required healthy measures of back-and-forth satire in countless individual and unique circumstances. Most ingenious were their nicknames. In almost all circumstances, they were not intended to be complimentary. They usually resulted from a worker with the best of intentions finding himself in a hapless and somehow embarrassing situation. All this took was a close-up observer whose supplied translation furnished a nickname with a story never to be forgotten.

What, for all practical purposes, was forgotten was the shop dog's given first name. While the nickname eventually became a merit badge, our dad scrupulously avoided receiving one and was referred to by his initials, J.C.

The Soo Line Bull

The shop dogs called him the Soo Line Bull, or Bull for short, as he once worked as a rail yard policeman for the Soo Line Railroad. He was a large, powerful man and was bull-like in his personality. His name that was never spoken was Charlie Petroff. Occasionally at lunchtime, he would pull a whole cooked chicken from his lunch pail, tear it in two with both hands and start eating each half.

Sometime each winter, he would travel "down below" (Twin Cities) to the Northern Pacific Hospital in Saint Paul, which the NP provided as an employee benefit to its workers. The Bull arrived with some or other reported ailment and extended his stay by how he represented his path to recovery. The hospital probably was warmer and more comfortable than his farmhouse. The food met his liking and was free. At some point, the Bull would inform the nurses and doctors he felt fine, would check out and be on his way back to Brainerd. The next winter, he checked into the hospital with a new back pain or stomach ailment.

One afternoon, after a number of winter hospitalizations at the NP, a few doctors and a nurse examined him and then walked outside the door. One of the doctors remarked loud enough to be heard inside his room, "We'll have to operate on Mr. Petroff in the morning."

In the dark of night, the Bull slipped out of the hospital and headed back to Brainerd, never again traveling "down below."

Blue Louie

Louie Jelacic always seemed down on his luck and bellyaching about everything to anybody he could get to listen. When any shop dog came to work with problems, they were told to go talk to Blue Louie, and then he would feel better. One shop dog claimed he made it a point to see Blue Louie once a week—the way some people make appointments with their psychiatrist.

Chicago Pete

In any shop dog conversation of some length, Chicago Pete couldn't help but relating the topic to something about Chicago. These guys worked in a somewhat close environment, and similar to a family, they knew accommodation was an important necessity, as their social banter made them better in handling their sometimes tough work situations. Routine was important. So Chicago Pete's banter just fit right in.

A recently hired worker also fit right in the work pattern. A month went by, and in a conversation the newly hired guy had with a longtime shop dog, Chicago Pete's name came up. The new worker asked the old-timer how many years Chicago Pete lived in Chicago. "He went there to spend two weeks with his brother many years ago," he answered, "then he came back here. But he's been talking about Chicago ever since."

HEAVY CARGO

His name was Sherman Potter. He claimed he flew heavy cargo planes in World War II. When his weight reached over three hundred pounds he was called Heavy Cargo Potter. Heavy Cargo died less than a month after he retired, and everyone really felt bad—he died before receiving his first retirement check.

THE SOCIAL OUTCAST

Martin Wenker worked on one of the welding crews in the car shops. In contrast to many of the workers, who were typical blue-collar men in their dispositions, Martin sat apart from the others at lunchtime and read a book of some intellectual interest to him. His demeanor just didn't mix with the typical shop dogs. In a frank moment, he told one of the welders who seemed sympathetic that he was a "social outcast."

Martin was a somewhat short and slender guy. His wife, Zita, worked at the Brainerd Public Library. She had a rather sturdy figure. Martin was not a very good welder, and his welds had bumpy profiles, called "grapes" by other welders, rather than the typical smooth joints. He was ill suited for blue-collar work. My brother Bill observed if the women's movement had happened in the '50s, his wife would have been the welder and Martin would have been the librarian, and both would have been happy with their reassigned workplaces.

Martin wrote the notices for the union meetings that were posted on bulletin boards in the car shops. He always wrote over the heads of his coworkers, who had basic working-class reading skills. Our dad brought one of his union meeting notices for us that announced the date and time of the meeting and included the statement "numerous cogent matters will be cogitated."

HIGH-RISE HOUSEMAN

Sometime around the mid-1960s, the City of Brainerd built two eight-story apartment buildings overlooking the Mississippi River as housing for senior citizens. They were the first real multistory apartment buildings in Brainerd. The only other apartments were in the second floors of retail stores in the downtown area. Typical Brainerd residents could apply for one of the high-rise apartments during the year they reached their sixty-fifth birthday. The railroad guys didn't think much of these apartments because they could not imagine living someplace that did not have a yard, garage and the continuing upkeep that shop dogs welcomed.

Harold Houseman's wife wanted to move into one of the apartments when Harold was first eligible—in January of that year—even though Harold would not be eligible to retire until later in the year. Harold and his wife moved in sometime in early January, but Harold did not tell any of his coworkers, who would have ridiculed him for moving into an apartment. One day a shop dog was driving past the building and saw Harold leave the apartment building with his lunch bucket under his arm. When Harold got to work, the boys greeted him with his new name—High-Rise Houseman.

HUNGRY BORG

Most people in Brainerd donated their unused clothes, kitchens items, tools and similar items to the Salvation Army, Good Will or Bethany House. Not the shop dog. When a worker had something surplus, they always checked with one of their coworkers to see if anyone needed or knew neighbors who could use the items and would want them. There was one guy who took everything offered. They called him Hungry Borg.

GIMPY FLANSBURG

Gimpy had an interesting penchant for malapropisms, but definitions were not his strong suit.

Leading up to the time when the Northern Pacific was planning to merge with other lines to become one railroad company (the Burlington Northern), the shop dogs talked a lot about how a merger could affect their jobs. Gimpy commented, "If the Great Northern and Northern Pacific submerged, a lot

A shop dog adjusting machinery. *Minnesota Historical Society.*

of jobs could be demolished." When the merger was finally in place and a pay raise was about to be granted, Gimpy asked if the pay raise would be "radioactive."

One very cold winter morning when he came to work, he mentioned the very cold "windshield" in the air. During the Vietnam War the guys heard the term *guerrilla warfare* used to describe the ground war. Gimpy was listening to the discussion and was a bit confused by the term. He asked one of the guys how they could train gorillas to shoot a rifle.

Bill remembers our dad remarking about Gimpy wearing sunglasses, saying that his eye doctor had just given him "Cadillac" surgery. He also mentioned meeting Gimpy downtown after they retired. Gimpy said that he had a heart problem and was taken to Brainerd Hospital and was in the "extensive care" unit for a few days and then transferred to a hospital in St. Cloud where they had "better tools."

LORD WHEELBARROW

A sweeper with an English accent had a wheelbarrow, broom and dustpan and swept the floors. Considered English nobility at the shops, he was called Lord Wheelbarrow.

KING GEORGE

George Hanson came to work in a suit and tie every day, as he wanted his neighbors to think that he was part of management. When he got to work, he put coveralls over the suit and tie and donned his welded underframes. When he finished work for the day, he would take off the coveralls and walk out of the shops in his suit and tie. He was called King George.

PANSY

How did Pansy Norquist get his nickname? Pansy was not very handsome—and he had a ruddy complexion.

CORDUROY JOHNSON

Corduroy Johnson worked in the storeroom office and wore the same corduroy jacket for many years.

YA YA

Ya Ya also worked in the storeroom. His name might have been Bob Enders. When he agreed with you, which he did 100 percent of the time, he would say, "Ya, ya!" and smile. The shop dogs remarked the words *ya ya* were about 10 percent of his total vocabulary.

PREACHER BEDAL

Preacher Bedal got his name from his clothes—he dressed for work in black pants, white shirt, black tie, black coat and black hat.

WALLEYE

Howell Laughton had one glass eye. His nickname was "Walleye" because the glass eye veered a bit to the left.

One day, Howell approached the drinking fountain and bent over slightly to bring his head close to the spout. But as he bent his head, one of his fellow shop dogs playfully attempted to slap him on his back, instead hitting the back of his head. Howell's glass eye popped out and fell through the drain into the U-shaped trap pipe below. Attempts to use a wrench to remove the drainpipe were thwarted by stuck threads.

"Somebody get Jim Rehberger!" another shop dog shouted. Jim walked up to the group to survey the situation. He saw my dad among the welding crew. Welders wore special bib overalls with a long narrow leg pocket that held thin, sixteen-inch-long welding rods. Jim asked our dad for a welding rod. "Anybody have chewing gum?" he asked.

One of the shop dogs pulled a wad of gum from his mouth and handed it to Jim, who stuck it on the end of the welding rod and slowly lowered the rod down the drainpipe until it came to the bottom of the U-shaped trap. Jim carefully raised the rod and turned it toward Howell, who picked the retrieved eyeball off the wad of gum on the rod, wiped it off on his sleeve, licked it a bit and inserted it back in his eye.

COTTON TOP

This was a name given to a shop dog who was albino and had a full head of curly white hair.

WASH TUBS

This shop dog was short enough that he had to stand on a washtub to use the sink.

Workers preparing to hang a sign. *Minnesota Historical Society.*

STUBBS SMITH

Every railroad payday, Stubbs Smith performed his customary payday walk out of the railroad shops' main entry gate, proceeding westward toward downtown Brainerd. Walking along Laurel Street, Stubbs would approach Seventh Street, with the Citizen's State Bank across the street along this shop dog's intended path. This was the moment when Stubbs would pull out a cigar stub from the left upper pocket of his well-worn jacket and then a matchbook from his right. He'd strike a light to his cigar and give it a few starting puffs until its smoke swirled noticeably in the air around him, as he passed, in public view, in front of the sober-faced granite facade of the bank building. Passing the bank, in front of the adjoining business storefronts, Stubbs stubbed out his cigar and put it back in his jacket pocket. His simple act of ever so temporary nobility was now finished—to be repeated the following payday and many more paydays to follow.

8

MORE SHOP DOGS

HJELMER ERICKSON

Hjelmer Erickson was assigned to the shops storeroom and occasionally ordered two of many parts, one for the railroad and the other one for himself. When he filled his garage, he built a huge cement block building to hold the overflow. He even took home a welding device even though he didn't know how to use it. Because Hjelmer was not handy enough to use any of these tools, the shop dogs considered him to be stealing. His wife, Pearl, used some of them to build an addition on their house. He would sit in the shade under a tree and watch her work. But with the passage of the afternoon when the tree no longer blocked the sun, Pearl would move his chair in the shade, Later, when he would be in sunshine again, Hjelmer would ask Pearl to move his chair back in the shade.

C.C. PETERSON

Clayton Carlyle Peterson drove a forklift and reputedly may have been DWI much of the time. C.C. had a part-time bartender job, but at the shops, he could fall asleep standing up. Everyone said that C.C. had a real talent—he could lock his joints when he slept upright. One time, he stood asleep leaning against a truck crane, and when the crane was moved, he was still standing.

A shop dog machinist. *Minnesota Historical Society.*

JOHNNY HARTMAN

Johnny Hartman was not the most knowledgeable guy at the railroad. Somehow management got him assigned to the NP union activities. Using his role in union negotiations, he somehow traded cost of living for a day off on the anniversary of the day the worker started working at the railroad—an unwise choice. At the shops, advancement was based strictly on seniority and certainly not intelligence. When the former materials man retired, Johnny's seniority placed him in charge of materials management.

Boxcars were built according to an NP determined program, such as two hundred boxcars built at a time. The number of boxcars to be built each day was usually eight under normal working conditions. The "materials man" would begin his workday by walking out of the car shops building with the forklift driver to a large materials yard and checking the stacks of various boxcar components. They would verify the number of each component needed that workday.

The driver determined how he could maneuver his large-sized machine through the stacks. He would unload the components in the shops building along the assembly process. As the boxcar program progressed, the various stacks of steel parts would gradually diminish.

One afternoon in the latter stages of a boxcar program, a few shop dogs sauntered out of the building for a smoke break. These were typically times they would see the diminishing stacks of material. This time, however, the guys saw a noticeable pile of boxcar interior braces, apparently not within Johnny's accounting system and not installed. No boxcars were found to be structurally unstable or functionally inefficient, but nonetheless NP conducted a search all over the western states to bring them back into the car shops for installation of the braces.

At some point, the number of boxcars built each day dropped from eight to five, and sometimes four, due to Johnny's inability to spot the parts where needed. The shop dogs came up with a solution. One of them humorously told Johnny he needed to use "paperwork" like the office workers did in their jobs. What Johnny needed to do was write down the component name on a slip of paper, then give them to the forklift driver, who obviously didn't need the slips of Johnny's paper—he knew where the parts in the yard were and the assembly line locations where the components needed to be spotted anyway.

As for Johnny, he kept his paper under his cap. He would take off his cap and give the driver one of the paper pieces, who would throw it away. The guys would find Johnny's paperwork scattered here and there around the shops. But most important, Johnny continued to be the materials man; the forklift driver could do his work the way it was needed, and the number of boxcars built returned to eight a day.

Eventually Johnny came to realize he was sixty-five and ready to retire. He went into the main office and filled out a retirement application. On his way out of the office, he saw the railroad superintendent, Kermit Knudson, a very gentle and kind-hearted gentleman. Johnny told Kermit about his upcoming retirement, and Kermit gave Johnny a perfunctory compliment by saying he would miss him.

Walking a short distance from the office, Johnny came back into the office and shredded up his application in front of the clerk, and to the dismay of his fellow shop dogs, he continued his bumbling work for another five years.

RUDY MILLOCH

The shops had the right job for Rudy. All day long, he sat on an upturned empty nail keg with a large anvil in front of him. Along his right would be a large pile of bent railroad spikes, delivered by an end loader. Rudy held a ten-pound sledgehammer in his right hand and with tongs in his left, he gripped a bent railroad spike that he would position on the anvil. With a brawny swing or two with his sledgehammer, he would straighten the spike, tossing it into a pile of now useable straightened spikes at the left side of him.

Position, swing, pound, toss, repeat. All day. The job fit his ability. When the pile of bent spikes was nearly depleted, an end loader driver scooped up the completed handiwork and dumped another load of crooked spikes. Like the Greek myth of Sisyphus eternally pushing his boulder uphill, Rudy's hours at the anvil turned into days, weeks, months and years.

In addition to straightening railroad spikes, he once was given another task. He became a temporary mailman. Previously, the railroad had Hjelmer Erickson delivering mail to twelve buildings, but Hjelmer was constantly seen holding up the envelopes to the sun and trying to read them and then gossiping about the information he gleaned around the shops. The solution was to have Rudy deliver the mail, since he could not read. Jo Thompson in the front office would sort the mail for Rudy with rubber bands around the packet of mail for each stop. Rudy would then step out and deliver the mail.

One day Rudy slipped on the ice and fell. The mail was strewn all over the ground. Rudy picked up the mail and immediately went back to Jo Thompson. She re-sorted the mail and put them in order, and Rudy was off to complete his route. The superintendent managed to find a replacement for Rudy, much to his relief.

OTTO BECK

The railroad unions were fairly strong, so that any work deemed obsolete allowed the affected workers to somehow remain at work. Otto Beck was a sheet metal worker, much needed in the days of wood boxcars. At some point, sheet metal had been eliminated with the introduction of steel boxcar construction. But union rules allowed Otto to stay on the job until his retirement.

Just for a joke, someone asked Otto to make a funnel. Otto carefully crimped the sheet metal in accordance with its slightly tapered shape. When he finished, somebody counted the hours he took and the almost negligible cost of the sheet metal. They told Otto that the total cost was many times what could be purchased at a hardware store for fifteen cents. Otto insisted this was a better funnel.

The dinnerware Otto's wife, Louise, set on their supper table was made by Otto, also out of railroad sheet metal.

CLYDE COOK

Clyde Cook's farmland was filled with huge boulders left by an ancient glacier, making his farm difficult to grow crops. One of his coworkers humorously suggested if he waited for winter, he could sell it as a sheep farm.

Clyde Cook took his vacation time in the summer. With his railroad pass for himself and his family, they would board the passenger train in Brainerd heading out west. The ever so pragmatic Clyde brought along some bags of apples and popcorn along with jugs of water. They rode the rails and stayed on the train for the three-day trip to Tacoma, Washington,

Jim Roscoe (*fifth from left*) with shop dogs in front of a late 1920s Ford. *Author's collection.*

where the train "dead-ended." The Cook family may or may not have left the passenger car to wander around the station platform for the two hours or so while railroad operations changed engines. Three days later, their vacation ended back in Brainerd.

BERT EIDE

JCPenney was the store in downtown Brainerd where the shop dogs bought their work clothes. Buying work clothes was an utterly straightforward process. No whimsical musing or apparel evaluation was necessary. Just finding the same shirts, pants, coveralls, jackets and caps to replace their clothing that was now worn out, as they did so many times, and prepared to complete the process.

In Penney's work clothing department, all that was required by a shop dog was selecting one's size. Henry, the clerk, would grip the end of a wide paper roll at the end of a broad counter mounted horizontally on a pair of brackets with a horizontal cutting strip. He would give it a quick, hefty pull and neatly rip off the right size paper sheet and lay it on a wide table. After payment was finished, Henry put the new clothing on the paper sheet, rolled them up and tied strings around the roll.

One Saturday morning, Bert walked into Penney's. Bert's daughter's wedding would take place in the late afternoon. Now he needed a suit. Wandering to the suit rack, Henry knew Bert needed a little help. Right away, color was unimportant to Bert, but Henry used his judgment to ascertain the size Bert needed. For the first time perhaps since his own wedding a long time ago, Bert was asked to try on the trousers and suit jacket. This time, he was a bit bewildered that the trousers' legs were very long and didn't have any cuffs.

Henry instructed Bert that he would roll up the leg material inside his pants and pin them up at the correct cuff length. When that was done, Henry informed Bert his suit would be ready in a week. Bert was astonished and told Henry about his daughter's wedding that afternoon. He seemed to expect Henry would roll up a ready-to-wear suit in a paper wrapper just as he always did with his work clothes.

Henry told Bert, "In that case, Bert, we'll leave the pins in for now. And with all of the fuss that the wedding will take, nobody will notice these tiny pins if I repin them more carefully."

Jim Roscoe (*center*) with other railroad workers. *Author's collection.*

The next Monday, Bert told the shops guys about how proud he was of his daughter and that he liked her new husband. He also casually mentioned his trouser cuffs situation and how quickly that worked out. Later, out of earshot, one of the shop dogs said, "The next time Bert needs to wear that suit, his casket will hide those pins."

9

LEGENDARY SHOP DOGS

JIM REHBERGER

Jim Rehberger was the guy who knew how to fix anything—a great practical problem solver who sometimes the foremen and technical engineers depended on. One day, Jim was called on to examine a guy with a very painful toothache. Jim sat him on a nail keg and then asked someone for his rivet tongs. He reached in and pulled the tooth out. Then he asked if someone nearby happened to have a half pint on them. Some whiskey was used to wash out his mouth with a dose of nonmedicinal pain reliever.

SCOOP SWANSON

Slipp's Hardware on Laurel Street in downtown Brainerd was owned and operated by Ed Slipp, who greeted most of his customers walking in the store by their first names. Noontime was busy for Ed. However, as the years moved along, the store became quiet after the noon hour. Ed would remove his striped work apron and roll it up to make his pillow for a short nap. Ed napped on his sheet metal main counter for a half hour or so.

Many of the shoppers at Slipp's Hardware were longtime customers. During Ed's nap time, a customer coming in would pick out what he needed, quietly put down money on the counter to pay for his purchase and then write down on a sheet of paper with an accompanying pencil his name, what he bought and the payment amount. These were the years long before sales taxes. If the customer paid for his purchase with several dollars above the tag price and needed change, he would pick the amount from the other change left by preceding customers.

One Saturday afternoon, shop dog Mike Swanson came in to buy a scoop shovel. As he came up to the napping Ed Slipp, an unfortunate event occurred. Mike was known for his honesty and his longtime faithful service as an usher at the First Lutheran Church. However, at this moment, he somehow fell into temptation. He quietly began to step out the door with the scoop shovel.

But Mike did not notice a downtown store clerk in a back area of the store. He saw Mike in the act of his misdeed. The police were called. Mike was arrested, taken to the police station, charged and released.

The next Monday morning in the shops workplace, a few workers assessed a task to be performed. One of them commented they needed one more man. One of them said, "Let's get Scoop to help us." The others laughed in immediate recognition of another one of them gaining a dubious nickname.

Once a shop dog was given a nickname, it became an indelible identifier for him to the rest of his working days and fixed into the shared camaraderie of everyone around him. After his death, a *Brainerd Daily Dispatch* obituary described him as Mike "Scoop" Swanson. His nickname outlived him.

Years later, when Swanson's wife passed away, the *Dispatch* obituary noted her as the wife of Michael "Scoop" Swanson.

STU KUNDE

Stu Kunde was the intellectual leader of the car shops. Stu worked in the materials section. He was revered for his World War II experience as a pilot in the navy. He subsequently joined the navy reserves and flew on weekends once a month for many years. He frequently told his coworkers when his weekend duty would include a flight over Brainerd. Everyone would wait for the plane to come, and Stu would tip the wing of the plane when he went over the car shops.

Our dad was helping his brother-in-law Ervin Lyman work on the exterior of his house in Duluth's west end neighborhood and told Stu that he would be in Duluth on Saturday. Dad told Stu the location of Ervin's house. Stu flew down the main drag of Duluth, found Ervin's house location and tipped the wing high over the Ervin's house. Our dad was the proudest person in Duluth that afternoon.

WILLY SCHLEIPPER

After World War II, many German people with important occupational skills immigrated to the United States. Willy Schleipper, a tall, handsome former German navy submarine crew member, became a Brainerd resident. Willy brought his family, who became friends with many people. Willy gained work at the car shops and was well liked by everyone.

One lunch hour, the guys began talking about who had traveled the farthest from Brainerd, excluding military service. Most had not ventured far away from Crow Wing County. A few shop dogs had been as far away as Chicago; several of them had been to Florida, and several visited family members who had moved to California. Someone asked if anyone had been to the nation's largest city, New York. Nobody responded. After a pause, Willy mentioned he had "seen" New York. Everybody knew without further discussion that during the war Willy must have had his turn at his German submarine's periscope off the coast of New York City.

PHIL TRIBER

Phil Triber, for all of his idiosyncratic traits, had no nickname. Well-liked by all the shop dogs, Phil Triber was notorious as a storyteller, and he just couldn't help himself from invariably stretching the truth with tall tales. Phil had lived in Devil's Lake, North Dakota, before moving to Brainerd. He said that his house settled every year and he had to jack the house up and add a layer of cement blocks to the foundation. When he left to move to Brainerd, his basement was twenty-eight feet deep.

When Phil Triber's daughter was in the hospital, Phil said he had to go to the shops to get some oxygen tanks because the hospital ran out. She had some broken bones, and they had to put pulleys and weights on her joints. But Phil claimed the weights were too heavy when she was hoisted to the ceiling. When Phil stepped in her hospital room and didn't see her, he shouted out, "Where are you, baby?" She answered, "Up here, Daddy!"

Phil Triber was an avid hunter. One fall, he was out hunting ducks. A flock flew over, and Phil fired at them. As he told the incident, he had been cleaning his shotgun and forgot to take out the cleaning rod. His shot threaded two ducks.

He was out deer hunting with friends when he spotted a buck. Phil fired and hit the deer. He tracked the deer through the woods and found it lying in a clearing. According to Phil, when he walked up to it to slit its throat, he climbed over the deer's back, and the deer jumped up. Phil took advantage of the opportunity and grabbed the deer's horns, steered the animal and rode it back to the hunting camp, where he did cut its throat. But Phil realized that when he had jumped on the deer, he had set down his rifle. Phil had to walk eleven miles back to where he jumped on the deer to pick it up and then walked back to camp.

Phil Triber always had a way of upping the ante on anything that happened of some consequence. One morning the guys were talking about a bad thunder and lightning storm the prior evening. Phil said his house was hit by lightning and burned out his TV so thoroughly that he could look through the screen and see the back wall behind it.

Phil Triber's son John worked in a shipyard and was later assigned to be a crew member on the same ship as his father during the war. At sea, during a storm when the ship was in trouble, the captain told John, "You take over, John—you built her!" John Triber was awarded so many medals during his World War II service that he could not put them all on his uniform—he filled his pockets with some of them.

RUDY LINDBERG

Almost all shop dogs took home only what they needed. Rudy Lindberg possessed a grander vision—and a business acumen. Part of his job in the storekeeping department was to distribute minor supplies to various departments in the Brainerd shops system and to outfit a supply train that distributed miscellaneous components to the railroad's outlying departments along the railroad's westward track.

Occasionally bulk quantities of lumber, dimension steel, paint, adhesives, barrels, oxygen and acetylene tanks and various tools and hardware were loaded into these boxcars by Rudy and his helpers. A local house mover who had a large truck with long steel beams and a multiwheel assembly pulled the boxcars out of the gate to their intended destination. A certain nefarious distribution process followed.

Rudy managed to source thick, high-quality wool blankets with the flourished inscription "Main Street of the Northwest" used on passenger trains, which he gave out for Christmas presents. Rudy also ran a full-service retail operation out of his garage. He had on-site sales and home deliveries. Men could also place orders. Someone ordered paint brushes from Rudy, but got spooked when he delivered them with his order book in hand and wrote out a receipt for the purchase. The shop dog was afraid that Rudy's notebook could be used to trace his transactions and employees could get fired for purchasing from him. My brother Bill commented he didn't think that most workers liked Rudy—but in that blue-collar culture, no one would turn him in or report any wrongdoing to senior management. Workers would comment later on how he stole the railroad blind and ended up blind.

Rudy helped organize supply trains that traveled a long section of the westward route and made his sales. Paint was the big seller on Rudy's supply trips. After about four or five of his trips, the landscape along the route showed barns and other outbuildings painted in Tuscan red, at that time the standard color of NP freight cars. Tuscan red worked well as a typical barn color.

When Rudy applied for retirement, what soon followed before his last day was an event that became a legend later known in Brainerd shop dog history as "Rudy's Last Ride."

The guys noticed the supply train was being loaded well beyond its normal complement. The word was out that Rudy was planning a caravan along part of its typical route. Normally shop dogs avoided being assigned to the supply train, as that would take them away from home for many days. Now they knew this train trip was not to be missed.

Bill worked with Buster Borders, who was on Rudy's final trip. Buster said that it was by far Rudy's biggest event—shovels, rakes, hammers, nails, paint brushes and similar tools were popular sales items. The train stopped at Twelve Mile Corner outside Brainerd, and farmers drove up from many directions and bought supplies from Rudy as his fists became flush with cash. Outside Wadena, thirty miles down the line was a similar stop. Several stops later, Rudy reached his last sale. The rest of the load was scheduled for railroad use for the remainder of the trip.

None of the shop dogs knew how he got away with these misappropriations, suspecting he had been bribing someone in the storeroom. But they did know Rudy was not getting rich. He played poker every weekend and was known as a poor card player.

ANOTHER SHOP DOG OF LEGEND: NELS PETERSON

The name Nels Peterson was very familiar around the shops, yet no shop dog had that name. One or more stories recounted were of a neighbor who didn't work at the shops helping a shop dog with the repair of a lake cabin.

"These cars made complete by the men in this picture." 1948. *Photo courtesy of Crow Wing County Historical Society; from Brainerd Lakes Area Photo Scanning Project.*

The neighbor saw a tool with the initials NP on the side of the steel tool. This was not uncommon.

On several of our dad's basement workbench tools were the initials NP— on a hammer, a few chisels, a coping saw and other miscellaneous tools. I was bequeathed a "Nels Peterson" chisel. In my tool collection today, I have a nail punch: a five-inch-long steel octagonal shaft with a tapered point end. The initials NP are faintly visible.

10

SHOP DOG TERMS

General Terms

Nickel Foreman

This was a lead position that paid five cents more an hour than the regular workers.

Hard Ones

Tobacco companies produced cigarettes in cardboard packs. These were called "hard ones." Shop dogs, like many other working-class men, made cigarettes from a bag of tobacco and a packet of very thin papers and hand-rolled them.

Mothers' Day

The shop dogs called payday "Mothers' Day," as many of their wives handled household finances. On payday, most of the guys brought their paychecks home, and they would head downtown to their bank to cash their paychecks. Some guys cashed them at the bar they faithfully patronized and immediately paid their bar bill.

It was common at that time to buy things on credit, which in those days meant trust or at least an understanding between merchant and customer. This understanding existed over not only bar counters but also many store counters when customers didn't have the money to buy supplies outright, especially before paydays. Settling up would occur, at least in part, after paychecks were cashed. Our sister, Mary, recalls,

> *I distinctly remember paydays. Payday came every two weeks—I remember there was a stretch a few days before payday. Mom would be a little more inventive with what she put together for lunch or dinner on those days. On payday, mom picked up dad from the shops. I sat in the back seat. The first stop was depositing his check at the bank. Then we stopped at the gas station and Dad would get gas, pay his bill and catch up on any news. Then we would go to Murphy's grocery store....Myrtle Murphy took out the cashbook with our name on the spine, and Mom paid our bill.*

Mary also remembers, "On pay days we would have chocolate marshmallow snowballs for dessert."

If finances and time were extremely tight, some shop dogs' paydays followed a unique method. The railroad shops property that faced a city street had a wood fence, approximately six feet high. Vertical flat boards formed a basic barrier. Over time, these boards shrunk in width, making thin vertical crevices that proved wide enough to slide a paycheck through. Some shop wives wanted to beat the typical busy downtown on shops payday. At an agreed-on time, a shop dog's wife would stand outside the fence by a particular crevice. The shop dog would call out her name, and she would respond. The husband would slide the paycheck partially through the fence until he could feel the tug of her hand. He would release the check and presumably hear a quick "Thank you."

Hair Burners

Hair burners were downtown women's hairdressers, so named for the effects of permanents and curling irons.

The Hundred Dollar Club

Once in a while, a shop dog driving under the influence would veer up on the boulevard and knock down an electrical power pole. The police would assess a fine for pole replacement of a hundred dollars. In a short time, various shop dogs would eventually know about it and assign him to be a member of the Hundred Dollar Club. It would become known by the shop dogs who "bought a particular pole," and his name would be figuratively attributed to it.

A Shop Dog Office Worker

A neighbor of ours carried a rather high opinion of himself. He claimed to his neighbors his work at the shops was office work. After work one evening, his boots were encrusted with dried concrete. Our dad told our neighbor Swanny Erickson, "They must have poured the floor in the office today."

The Blueberry Special

Diesel train cars provided passenger service to various communities throughout rural Minnesota areas, in an era when regional bus service was not yet available. The nickname for this dull black train car was the Galloping Goose. But on a day or two late in the summer, this train had a special name: the Blueberry Special.

Each late summer meant a trip up north to pick blueberries. Railroad families would board a diesel-powered train car with an engine up front and a long passenger area, carrying buckets, lunch and jugs of water. They disembarked at the location somewhere near Bemidji to gather the abundant blueberries. By the time they returned home to Brainerd, they were happy with their pickings, which were later put through the canning process, making preserves and jelly for winter.

Carry

When a shop dog was in a state of alcohol overload or hung over, another worker "carried" him by helping him to get his job done.

Carry Out

Surreptitious removal of railroad materials, usually in lunch pails. The typical railroad worker's lunch bucket had a limited life. Many shop dogs reinforced their lunch buckets with heavy hinges and closing latches so that heavier take-home items could be safely and surreptitiously transported. Our dad installed oversized hinges threaded with welding rod instead of the usual flimsier hinge pins and a reinforced latch on his lunch bucket.

Sometimes, a shop dog walking out the gate after work carried his lunch pail with his arm hanging noticeably lower, due to the weight of the lunch pail's illicit contents. Depending on what he was carrying out, however, the weight might exceed the strength of the handles. Our brother John remembers seeing this when he picked up our dad from work one day. Dad pointed this out.

> "Do you see the guy with the red cap just coming through the gate? He has his lunch pail tucked under his arm. You can bet that pail is loaded with something he pilfered from the shops." Another worker walked out wearing a heavy winter coat. "You can bet he is concealing something." He then told me the story about a guy who was exiting the shops with a heavy coat on in warm weather. He had wound a length of chain around his neck. The guard asked him to take off his coat, revealing the chain. "The guys must have hung it on me!" he exclaimed.

A shop dog might carry his thermos under his other arm to allow more space in the pail for what he was carrying out. It was common for a shop dog to carefully measure his new lunch bucket, using his folding ruler to determine its maximum capacity. Different materials involved different considerations. A shop dog with an open lunch pail once contemplated how much canvas could be packed inside. Another shop dog passing by stopped to advise him on the exact measurements. "That's all she'll hold," he said.

An important note here: The railroad workers considered these items as earned and not stolen. But taking more than they needed was not right. And those workers who did so were criticized, although out of earshot.

When the merger with Great Northern, Burlington and Santa Fe occurred in the 1980s, the new main rolling stock color became Cascade green. Northern Pacific's Tuscan red was a muted color and its red pigment was prone to fading. Cascade green was somewhat bright and resistant to fading.

Some of the shop dogs welcomed the new color that compared favorably to the somewhat dull reddish brown NP color. Cascade green found its way into shop dogs' aesthetics. Before long, shop dogs' house and garage trim, as well as trailers and birdhouses, were painted this color. One shop dog observed about its outsourced availability from the shops, "It's already brightened up Brainerd nicely."

PLACE NICKNAMES

The Apple Orchard

Certain places around Brainerd gained nicknames. Various railroad machinery items that required repair were taken to the scrap dock to dismantle their unusable parts. Much of the older machinery was dirty and greasy, and the shops assigned men to do this work who were not trainable to perform even the most minimally skilled tasks. The skilled workers designated the scrap dock as the "apple orchard" to confer the place with an intended faux respectability.

Mortgage Hill

An area on Brainerd's south side became built up with pretentious homes of the business community members. The shop guys called the area Mortgage Hill.

The Gallbladder Home

A local doctor developed a reputation and large income from treating many patients' routine intestinal issues by gallbladder removal. His extravagant residence gained the nickname the Gallbladder Home.

Boxcar Point

By the late 1950s, Brainerd shop workers were benefiting from an expanding economy that favored railroads. They had long seen the town's middle class enjoying summer lake cabin life around the shores of the myriad lakes north of Brainerd.

Approximately twelve miles southeast of Brainerd, South Long Lake had irregularly shaped lakeshore properties that were largely undeveloped. Shop workers took advantage of what the lake had to offer. One large point of land on the south side of the lake attracted several railroad men and their families. Eventually, shop workers bought most of these lots.

Typical railroad workers were adept at home repair. They loaded their trailers with salvaged boxcar lumber from the Apple Orchard, and they found used doors and windows. They procured paint from the shops and carried out tools in their lunch pails. The exterior envelope of their cabins was composed of basic shapes and simple gabled roofs. Almost all featured boxcar siding. The vertical siding nailed in place displayed interesting arrangements. Aligning strips of siding according to original logo and lettering was completely unimportant. What resulted were graphic fragments of randomly reconfigured iconography.

This area became locally known as "Boxcar Point."

Painting their cabins was to be done last, but whether this occurred varied by owner. Habitually task-driven shop dogs applied paint on boxcar siding sooner rather than later, but others prioritized catching fish. The unfinished painting that persisted and the cabin architecture created a unique and quixotic cabin vernacular known only to this locale.

Eideville

In the once distinctly rural area east of the shops area, one of the several Eide families cleared away a scattering of jack pines and built a house. Another Eide household settled nearby, later joined by a few other of their brethren. Whether it was due to the peculiarities of the Eides' method of house construction or the eccentricities of the Eides themselves, the shop dogs found a way to nickname their enclave Eideville.

The Stone Garden

A sign of shop dogs' pragmatism and success was to buy grave plots for themselves and their wives and pay for their own funerals. Evergreen Cemetery is roughly eight blocks north of the shops but did not escape a shop dog nickname. They called it the Stone Garden.

When one of the guys would mention his recent Evergreen Cemetery real estate purchase at lunchtime, the other men would quickly and audibly measure its distance to their plots. Then there came jocular comments such as, "Sonofabitch, I've had to work alongside you for these twenty-some years. So I'm going to have you planted near me for how in the hell long?"

Little Hollywood

Our uncle Dode drank a lot of beer seemingly with no effect. However, whiskey became his demon. He lost the ability to take care of his family. His work at the railroad eventually faltered and he lost the best job he could ever have. He sometimes stayed in a small misbegotten area of downtown near South Ninth Street and Front Street, euphemistically called Little Hollywood. It was made up of very small shacks where a local scattering of other similarly afflicted men were able to find places to sleep for a few nights. They would eat whatever food could come their way and invariably find booze. Some of these men could occasionally lean on the stability of their family members for temporary subsistence.

11

MORE SHOP DOG STORIES

Fat Fox

Once in a while, some shop dogs would place bets as to who would be the first one to get a barstool at the Winnipeg Bar on Front Street. These bets were typically good-natured. But Fat Fox would excessively brag to the guys around him when he was the first. One payday afternoon, a few of the guys got a forklift driver to drive into the parking lot and hoist up Fox's car by the rear bumper. They slipped a pair of concrete blocks under the rear axle. The forklift driver slowly lowered the car and retreated to his workstation. The rear tires were left a little over an inch from the pavement. The guys went up to Fox and placed big bets with him.

The next morning, Fat Fox said nothing about it.

Getting Limed

Another celebrated prank involved a shop dog whose son was in the Little League. The shop dog was in charge of "liming," laying down a four-inch-wide white strip of powdered lime on the base lines of the baseball field. For game days, he would take home a lunch bucket filled with lime powder. One day, a couple of minutes before four o'clock, one of the guys surreptitiously opened the lunch pail and set it on its side. He placed a shallow tin of water inside the pail alongside the bed of lime powder and closed the latch. When the whistle blew, the shop dog grabbed the handle of the lunch pail, flipping it upright as he left the shop. By the time he walked near the gate where the watchman stood by, the activated clouds of lime were foaming from the vents, so he had to put the lunch bucket under his jacket.

Wearing a Push Broom

Harry Nelson could have bought a broom handle at Slipp's Hardware for nineteen cents. But one day just before the four o'clock whistle, Harry took a push broom apart from its handle, loosened his belt and slipped the brush under the waistband of his pants. He then lifted the handle to the back of his neck and slid it down under his shirt. He felt the broom handle moving down his back. He tucked it under his belt and guided it down his left pants leg to just above his ankle. By this time the whistle blew to end the workday. Harry started out, his right leg bending at the knee and swinging his stiff left leg as he moved toward the shops gate. He was sure the watchman would think he had an injured leg.

At the gate, a mischievous shop dog tripped him. Harry slipped and fell but couldn't get up. A number of shop dogs were in the know about the broom handle and walked around him grinning as they passed by. Finally, Carl Palmquist, who read the Bible during lunch hour, performed a provident deed and helped him to his feet, and Harry was on his way home.

How Bennie Karls Got His Eyeglasses Broken

Bennie Karls was a real troublemaker, picking on and provoking the younger employees. One day in the 1950s, he started in on a new employee. The enraged new employee hit him in the face and broke his glasses. Bennie complained to the superintendent and claimed that his new thirty-five-dollar glasses were broken. The new employee was called in and told to reimburse Bennie or he would be fired. The employee did not have the thirty-five dollars and told his coworkers that he really needed the job.

The shop dogs decided to take up a collection. They opened a lunch bucket and asked guys to throw in their change to help the new guy pay for Bennie's glasses. Bennie had difficult times with many of the guys he worked with, but there was a long line of men tossing money in the lunch bucket. At some point, they counted the money and had $110, so they had to turn away more offerings.

CARRYING OUT NAILS

Another legendary story is that a shop dog was building his house and regularly brought home various carpentry items in his lunch bucket. Many months later, walking through the gate, he accidentally dropped his lunch bucket and the lid fell open. Nails spilled all over the ground. He was immediately afraid he would be fired for stealing from the NP.

The watchman waved him through the gate and then told another watchman standing by, "Those nails are finishing nails for wood trim. So he is just finishing his house. If he would be fired, the railroad would probably hire a new guy who would soon be starting to build his house, so we would start this all over again."

POWER TO THE PEOPLE

Another story involved a shop dog house directly across the unpaved street from the power plant. One winter day, someone noticed the typically hard-packed snow had melted in a strip across the street leading from the power plant to a particular house. The shop dog had somehow tapped into a steam line from the power plant to heat his house.

SHOP DOGS WERE ALWAYS ON THE LOOKOUT

Otto and Louise Beck, a short and frumpy couple, looked like a pair of knickknacks on a curio shelf. They were amusingly well known for spending every evening dutifully patronizing the downtown Brainerd bars after the workday ended.

One fateful Saturday evening, our parents were home as they always were, watching Jackie Gleason. At about 9:00 p.m., the phone rang, and it was one of Dad's close shop dog friends. He and his wife were celebrating a milestone wedding anniversary, and he asked Dad for our mother and him to join them at the Eagles' Club. Knowing what our dad's response would be, he told our dad, "I knew you would say no, but we're saying get ready for the cab to pick you up in a half hour."

Early the next morning, as we were all getting ready to go to church, Dad was in a highly unusual and frustrated mood. "Goddammit! I wanted us to leave the Eagles earlier, but we couldn't get away," he muttered. "Then they

The shops building, south facade. *Minnesota Historical Society.*

called the cab for us so late in the evening, and the cab driver told us when we got in the car that he had one other couple to take home, and I just saw the whole goddamn thing that would happen. It was Otto and Louise."

Mom said, "Well, Jim, they are very nice people, and Otto was so friendly with you!"

Dad replied, now in a low but apprehensive voice, "Monday morning the guys will be laughing at me at work."

The next evening after work, he was in a light, easy mood at supper. With an ever so faint smile, he said, "So this morning I just knew somebody would have seen how we left the club. And sure as hell, nothing came for most of the morning. But then several of us were setting up our welding spots, and Frank Jordan tapped me on the shoulder and said, 'Jim, I hope you know how your kids will feel some morning when they see Louise in your kitchen frying bacon on the stove.'"

12

WORKING AT THE SHOPS

Railroad Workers and Unions

The two unions at the shops were the Brotherhood of Railway Carmen and the Brotherhood of Railway Clerks. According to my brother Bill, their main functions at the local level were to ensure that seniority (the workers nicknamed it "whiskers") was taken into consideration in all bargaining agreements. At union meetings, most discussions centered on protecting employee rights and handling grievances against management. An important concern was keeping a safe working environment.

Two publications came in our mailbox. The Brotherhood of Railway Carmen published the *Railway Carmen's Journal*, a "face" publication with a glossy cover and interior pages promoting various regional and national events with their members wearing suits lined up in several rows facing the camera. The other publication was *The Labor Paper*, a four-page newspaper in a plain format that served to advocate for labor rights in a decidedly militant, faintly Marxist manner. Our dad wanted me to make sure I read that paper.

At the national level, the unions had significant effect. The Railroad Retirement Act (RRA) replaced the Social Security Act for rail industry employers and provided monthly annuities for employees based on age and service or on disability. Originally passed in 1934, periodic amendments were made until the early 1970s.[26] Bill observed that pulling the railroad workers out of Social Security was no doubt their best undertaking. The railroad retirement was very generous and made the retirement years of

An aerial view of the railroad shops site. *Photo courtesy of Crow Wing County Historical Society.*

Administrators in the car shops building. *Minnesota Historical Society.*

the workers the best financial years of their lives. Throughout their working years, the majority of workers, like our parents, bought used cars, but in retirement they bought new ones. That meant that some railroad workers were making more in retirement than they did when they had worked.

During Bill's career working for the government in Washington, D.C., he worked with a woman whose grandfather was in Congress when the Railroad Retirement Act was passed. She said it provided for a generous retirement because Congress felt that the railroad workers were taken advantage of during the 1920s, '30s and '40s. What was also generous is that the spouse got half of the employee's retirement, even though she did not work at the railroad shops.

WORLD WAR II

During World War II, my dad remained working at the Brainerd shops. Railroad work was considered a national service. A railroad worker who had a family was exempt from the draft. Of the shop dogs who did enlist, the majority became soldiers in the army, although others chose the navy. Military service gave them the opportunity to experience a segment of their lives very separate from the town of Brainerd and the farm fields of Crow Wing County. During the war, some ex–shop dogs, now fighting men, managed to keep in touch with one another, at times facilitated through letter connections by their families.

As happened in millions of workplaces after the war, veteran shop dogs shared war stories over their lunch pails. Two shop dogs shared an especially deep connection. A shop dog was serving on a cruiser in the South Pacific that became involved in the Battle of the Coral Sea. His ship was hit with two torpedoes and began to sink. Another cruiser pulled alongside, and a relay line and pulley system with a leather seat was set up to connect both ships. When the shop dog was relayed to the cruiser, he was taken off the line on the rescuing cruiser by a shop dog he had worked with.

Sixty-four Brainerd soldiers served in the Philippines. Many became prisoners of war and experienced brutality and torture during the Bataan Death March. During the march, one Brainerd soldier collapsed. A former shop dog soldier picked him up and carried him to their prison camp. Half the Brainerd soldiers were killed or did not survive.[27] There is a Bataan Memorial in Brainerd commemorating those who served.

Summer Work at the Shops

In the 1950s and early 1960s, many railroad families found opportunities for their sons of high school age to work summers at the shops. As the oldest of the four of us, our parents held hopes I would follow high school graduation with attending a technical school. That would place me at an advantage when I would join the military, which could set my foundation for learning a trade. My dad was not the guy to give his sons career advice, but he once remarked to me, "Duke Carlson's kid went to a refrigeration school in Saint Cloud. I hear that's damn good money." They considered college was out of my consideration because I was more interested in cars, specifically tricking up the V-8 engines in my various successive Fords.

Most importantly, our parents did not want me working summers at the shops, for fear I would make the shops my working career. Our dad had achieved a railroad job as a means to rise above the stultified farm life they had experienced in farming areas southeast of Brainerd. Many shop dogs had bettered their lives through their jobs at the shops.

However, America had changed. The 1950s and '60s produced a diversified economy, and young people after high school began to seek college degrees. Many shop dog families raised sons and daughters who became doctors, lawyers and teachers who gave their parents great pride.

When my brothers, John and Bill, were in college and my sister, Mary, was planning her own college track, Bill wanted to work summers at the shops, and my parents now felt comfortable enough that he could work there. And I hasten to add that Bill's work at the shops bestowed him the honor of rubbing elbows with many shop dogs, enough for him to experience that status and acquire his memories today that have greatly contributed to my writing this book.

Of college students who took summer jobs, most were not rehired the next summer. Bill worked in the dismantling yard for three summers as a laborer. He remembers,

> *I was accepted by my coworkers partly because of Dad's reputation and the fact that I was raised in a blue-collar environment and I knew not to brag about college and how I would end up with a white-collar career. I was very comfortable in the blue-collar world. The other college kids did not seem to have the rapport with their coworkers that I did.*

This was significant. Bill had the instinct, and respect, not to insult shop dogs with dubious notions of bragging. And the shop dogs working with Bill gave him the honor of initiation into their ranks.

My work shoes got oiled the first week, and then a few weeks later, I went through the nail keg ritual. A nail keg had a one-inch lip projecting around the top and one of the guys would fill the top on the keg with water and then place a plywood board over the keg. You would be invited to sit down and just as you were getting into the sitting motion, the board would be pulled and you would sit in one inch of water and walk around the rest of the day with a wet ring on your butt for other shop dogs to see. I thought I really made it with the guys when a bunch of them took me out drinking after work to celebrate my twenty-first birthday.

13

SHOP DOG BENEFITS AND RETIREMENT

The steady economic strength of the railroad provided continuous longtime employment. Shop dogs worked full time, continually, except for a mid-1950s shutdown that the shop dogs nicknamed the "Eisenhower Recession" and that lasted several months.

Over the years, the Northern Pacific and the various employee unions settled into a series of accords that basically gave workers very livable but not generous pay. "The average shop dog was happy to be a railroad employee and there was little or no complaining about the work," remarked my brother Bill. "The shop dog was happy to have a job that paid well enough and was relatively secure." A shop dog who had earned "whiskers" (seniority) could look forward to a better salary. Our cousin Marilyn Anderson Jacobs recalls,

My father worked as a stationary engineer at the power plant at the NP shops for forty years, retiring just two years before his death. He was able to walk to work every day and carried a lunch pail to work. His coworkers were his friends, and he often spent time fishing with them. While fishing with one of his friends, he helped haul in a forty-pound Muskie. We have pictures of this huge fish, and needless to say, it was not a catch and release fish; it was food....I never knew how much he was paid per hour, but it was enough to support our family, and my mother did not have to work outside our home on a steady basis. My sister and I were able to go to college, and my parents paid for some of our expenses on his salary.

A 1950 retirement party in the tool room. *Photo courtesy of Crow Wing County Historical Society.*

OFFICIAL BENEFITS

An NP worker benefit was vacation—two weeks a year for employees with a specified number of working years and up to a month for more long-term workers. Most shop dogs split their allotted time into two periods per year. Their very pragmatic lives were used for house or car repair or extended daytime fishing or hunting. A few shop dogs amusingly remarked two vacation weeks at a time was enough—otherwise they might "run out" (of tools, bolts and other small hardware items).

Thanks to free train travel benefits, some shop dogs visited relatives living far from Brainerd. Increased vacation time was based on seniority. They could also obtain free NP passenger train travel for members of the immediate family in the NP system, extending from Chicago, across the Upper Midwest to Tacoma, Washington, on the West Coast. Marilyn remembers,

As a benefit of working for the NP railroad, our family enjoyed free travel by rail. Our family made a couple of trips to Oregon and Washington with free passes courtesy of the NP….I traveled back and forth to Duluth when I was in college on free passes.…In college in Duluth, we had to be careful to watch the weather, as if the train was late coming from the west, the train would be late coming into Brainerd and leaving at 5:00 a.m.

The NP also operated a hospital in Saint Paul where workers could take advantage for general purposes apart from job injuries, which included health issues occurring with the passage of life and advancing age, continuing after retirement and occasionally into a worker's final days.

Working at the Shops Afforded Shop Dogs Benefits That Were Unofficial as Well as Official

Trailer Hitches

In those days, a trailer was essential for hauling building materials, towing fish houses or taking home many gunnysacks filled with russet potatoes from Perlinger's farm west of Brainerd. It was common for Brainerd men in those days to drive a new car out of the dealership with a trailer hitch. Hitches came at an additional cost.

The shop dogs had another source for trailer hitches. A wall in the shops held samples of trailer hitches by car make: Plymouth, Chevrolet, Ford and so on. These could be "ordered" by shop workers and fabricated, free of charge, by the car shops' welding crew to custom-fit their vehicles.

Fish House Stoves

The railroad shop work crew also fabricated fish house stoves, custom-built per the shop dog's requirements. By the end of November, lake ice was thick enough to support a fish house. Occasionally, a shop dog would see another shop dog's fish house stove and notice an individual feature that his stove did not have. As a result, the welders would revise or replace his stove with that element.

A Shop Dog's Last Workday

A venerable NP railroad tradition happened on the last working day of a shop dog. His fellow workers would take up a collection out of respect for working with him. This became the final judgment and more of a tribute to the shop dog. Most of the collection was folding bills, but also according to tradition, a silver dollar was a sign of special respect. My brother Bill remembers our dad getting about $900, including many silver dollars.

Harold Ringer was an angry guy who nobody liked working with. Several hundred men were working at the shops at that time. However, the collection for Harold Ringer totaled $1.50. His son mentioned throwing in $1.00, but nobody would admit to throwing in the $0.50.

Also on the last day, some shop dogs took their thermoses out of their lunch bucket, put the metal bucket on the bed of a twenty-ton press and then pushed a button that flattened it out to an extremely thin sheet of metal. They then would throw it on a metal scrap pile and hand their thermoses to whoever needed it.

In their retirement, the shop dogs devoted their days to maintaining their houses. They also maintained their shop dog friendships. Some of them looked forward to weekends for lake cabin time. Many shop dogs set up regular monthly lunchtimes with the men they had worked with at a corner lunch café near the shops. Several social clubs, such as the Eagles and the Moose, became Saturday nights together. Fishing and hunting continued their friendships. And for those World War II combat veterans, remembering and recounting their experiences was of great importance.

But continuing updates of their sons and daughters and their grandchildren became most important. The retired shop dogs kept everybody up to date with how their families were doing. When a son or daughter got married, his newlywed spouse almost always came from a Brainerd family.

And very important, with the birth of a grandchild, the shop dog indulged in the ceremony of strolling around with a celebratory cane and gaining congratulatory handshakes.

Sometime later came visits to the hospital and the inevitable funeral.

His Last Whistle

Into retirement, the Northern Pacific Railroad took medical care of their workers into consideration. In terminal situations, the shop worker and his spouse would be transported to the Northern Pacific Hospital in Saint Paul to determine whatever care might extend his life or whether the end of his life was likely. Those very solemn situations were always known by the shop dogs, even to the day and hour of the shop dog and his family leaving Brainerd for the NP hospital.

Departure usually happened in early morning after the shops workday started. When the shops seven o'clock whistle sounded, someone would comment about him, "He just heard his last whistle."

14

ARE THE GLORY DAYS OF RAILROADING OVER?

THE DECLINE

The rise and decline of the Brainerd railroad shops represents the story of many industrial cities and towns throughout America. For decades, major industries became an enormous force in local economies. In many ways this bolstered the overall identity and well-being of towns and cities. This was evident in workplaces, in their neighborhoods, in downtown businesses whose income largely came from industrial workers' paychecks. City neighborhoods where worker families lived were stable communities. But decades on, factories and railroads, almost unnoticeably, began to decline in economic stature and in human capital. America's industrial base atrophied.

As the 1960s arrived, the departure of steam had left railroad towns and cities long before their citizens were aware of its demise. Most of these towns and cities had been formed with railroads providing everyday service.

Living in Brainerd during my youth, at the end of a working day, we were accustomed to see railroad workers carrying their lunch pails in simple rhythm on their way home. My dad walked nearly a mile to and from work. Nobody knew when the mournful whistles in the night would be heard no more, or when we could no longer experience the close-up hiss of steam or see the might of iron.

In 1970, the Northern Pacific Railroad put out the word of an upcoming merger. The Northern Pacific would merge with the Great Northern; the Chicago, Burlington & Quincy; and the Spokane, Portland & Seattle railroads.[28] According to the NP, it would have no effect on the Brainerd shops. But the shop dogs sensed the merger was executed to combine operations that would eventually cause diminishment of the Brainerd shops.

> *The locomotive shop, until 1955, did repair work for the whole line, but now repairs only its own yard engines. The Livingston, Montana shops, more centrally located for the line, has taken over this function. The blacksmith shop used to finish and assemble all locomotive wheels and axles for the line, as at one time, the special equipment required for that task was located only in Brainerd.*[29]

They knew it had been several years since a worker's retirement was filled by a new hire. They were aware that the era of powerful and active railroads across the nation was coming to a decline.

Every shop dog considered the shops more than a job and a paycheck. They paid close attention to news they heard from down below about the railroad's operations and its economic well-being. In the Brainerd shops, at first small cuts were made in basic operations; then, various departments in the shops were closed one at a time. Providently, the advanced age of the shop dog workforce allowed a slow reduction of the workforce without laying off seasoned veterans.

> *Employment here now approaches 270 men, plus 125 in the store department and up to fifty at the tie plant for an approximate total of 540. When comparing the current employment numbers with those of the late 1800s when close to 1,200 men were employed, it must be remembered that mechanization has changed employment patterns.*[30]

RAIL'S DIMINISHING PRESENCE

Railroads were the nation's primary source of freight transportation prior to 1930. In the decades afterward, railroads became adversely affected by the growing influence of trucks and the increased volume interstate highways provided. Railroads were losing their favored status, with lower financing and no longer having rights of way. "Furthermore, the government mandates that boxcars be removed from service when they are 50 years old. These combined factors mean that about 57% of the current boxcar fleet will be retired in the next 15 years, and orders for new boxcars stand at only 0.49% of all freight car orders."[31]

After World War II, the nation's growing population was starting to expand into the suburbs while being reduced in central cities. On the East Coast, these areas outside of city limits became known as "streetcar suburbs." Streetcars would become largely replaced in favor of buses and cars. Rail tracks lacing through many parts of our cities and countryside began to lose their silvery shine. Rails were being torn out of the ground.

Many suburbs eventually became municipalities to themselves. Much of their built areas had no recognizable downtowns or even sidewalks. However, these suburbs and their car-centered modes of living essentially invented the supermarket, shopping center and drive-ins of many types. In the meantime, urban downtowns began to lose their economic vitality, and some Main Streets became leftover places.

Moving and delivering freight by truck increased dramatically. By 1972, six major northeastern railroads went bankrupt. In the mid-seventies, the Consolidated Rail Corporation (Conrail) was formed as a government-funded private company, which struggled for years before finally finding stability. From that time until today, over 1,400 railroad tracks all over the nation have been removed. Today, in many outlying areas, tracks that remain reveal patinas of rust.

In many respects, the glory days of railroading are over. We no longer hear the hiss and see the smoke of steam-powered trains and hear only infrequently the insistent hum of diesel railroad engines. But today railroad nostalgia remains widespread. There have always been fans of all ages as well as history-minded enthusiasts.

> *Railroad boxcars are perhaps not only the best-recognized pieces of equipment ever put into service but also one of the most identifiable symbols of the industry itself....* [They have] *a history tracing back to the earliest years when railroads realized that some freight and lading needed at least a little protection from the outside elements and Mother Nature.*[32]

Railroads are deeply entrenched on the internet and throughout American music and culture. Songs such as "Mystery Train," "This Train Is Bound for Glory" and "500 Miles Away from Home" have been sung by music legends such as Leadbelly, Woody Guthrie, Bob Dylan and Johnny Cash. Songs of fabled train lines, such as "The City of New Orleans" and "Rock Island Line," are but a few, and trains figure greatly in songs such as "Folsom Prison Blues" and countless others.

15

THE BRAINERD SHOPS BUILDINGS
FACE THE WRECKING BALL

Burlington Northern's announcement that several significant buildings would be demolished foretold a grim and uncertain future for the shops site. Despite assurances that there would still be a small crew of workers on-site, the decision to tear down some of the buildings that had been integral to the purpose of the shops was rightly taken as a foreboding sign. It was also a threat to the site's intactness, which could compromise efforts to have the shops listed as a historic site.

The historic buildings, seven of which date to 1881 and one to 1871 have become costly white elephants, said Bob McGinnis, material manager at the shops. "They've out-lived their usefulness," he said.

History is one thing, McGinnis said. Economic survival is another. "They say we've got to save these majestic old buildings," he said. "Well, who is going to pay to maintain them?"

Burlington Northern intended to keep a few of its departments operating in the railyard. On a worksite that had employed over 1,000 workers at its maximum, there would be just 180 at the railyard. The operations would be consolidated on the northern side, consigning the whole of the south side to fates of abandonment and destruction....Many buildings were slated to be demolished. The railroad planned to tear down the boiler and machine shops, the main south storage building, the blacksmith's shop, the power plant, the paint and sign shops, the bridge and building headquarters, and the pattern shop.

All but the Power Plant were demolished.

The main building
office tower. *Minnesota
Historical Society.*

Although several of the remaining buildings on the site were eventually listed in the National Register of Historic Places, historic designation is considered to be honorific and provides no protection from demolition unless federal funds are involved, which was not the case here.

The railroad upgraded a few systems and did some important repairs on the remaining buildings. The railroad kept the surplus shed and planned to use the main car shops building as storage for the bridge and building department headquarters. The electricians would move to the main car storage building. Linemen, communication and signal maintenance workers would move to the downtown depot.

The iconic Tower administration building, built in 1871, would be spared. It would stand sentinel over a once-mighty railyard, awaiting fluctuating uses in the years ahead.

Many of the people of Brainerd did not want to see the Brainerd NP shops destroyed. While some may have been ambivalent, other people held deeply felt connections. Brainerd citizens know that their city would not have existed without the railroad. A great deal of Brainerd's population had some degree of relationship with the shops. They either had a family member or knew someone who had worked at or with the shops in some capacity.

By the 1980s, manufacturers and large industries had been closing down, relocating or taking their jobs overseas. In the decades previous, a worker could be sure of a job and a paycheck, and perhaps retirement—there was a mutually understood need between worker and company. Now these social contracts were being broken.

The railroad in Brainerd had experienced a merger in 1970 that resulted in a gradual reduction of its workforce, then a winding down of operations by 1985. The NP shops had been emblematic of Brainerd's growth and success. Then it became largely empty. Brainerd's residents understood how much the railroad was part of the city's identity. At some point, most of Brainerd's residents were connected in some way to the shops. There were railroad workers in families, or people had friends and neighbors whose jobs were at the shops, or had jobs connected in some capacity to the railroad. While there had been gradual slimming down of departments, and some parts of operations shifted to shops in other towns, this news struck hard.

When the news of the shops' proposed demolition spread, its endangered status struck chords with people in the historic preservation movement and other civic organizations in Minnesota. The importance of the Northern Pacific shops for Brainerd was a powerful example of place and time not only for Brainerd but also nationally. And as is often the case, a small group of historic preservationists began a course of action that would lead to the NP shops' historic status on local and national levels.

A continuance form (a type of nomination document) to the National Register of Historic Places prepared by architectural historian Norene Roberts, PhD, led to the consideration and eventual listing as a nationally

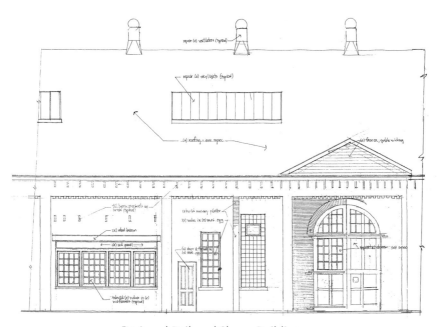

Brainerd Railroad Shops Buildings

A line drawing of the shops, side view. *Drawn by Bob Roscoe.*

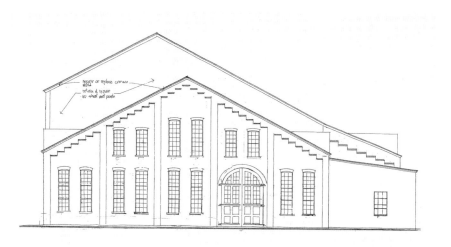

Brainerd Railroad Shops Buildings

Brainerd Railroad Shops Buildings

Top: A line drawing of the shops, front view. *Drawn by Bob Roscoe.*

Bottom: A line drawing of elevation sketches. *Drawn by Bob Roscoe.*

recognized historic district. During this process, the description of the NP shops' definitive historical merit was elaborated. As typical in a historic district, not every building in the district would merit historic consideration. But a sufficient number of buildings and other structures would qualify for designation as a historic district.

16

HISTORIC DESIGNATION
AND REUSE

Designation Process with
the National Register of Historic Places

The National Register is part of the National Park Service, whose parent department is the Department of the Interior. The mission statement on its webpage states:

> *The National Register of Historic Places is the official list of the Nation's historic places worthy of preservation. Authorized by the National Historic Preservation Act of 1966, the National Park Service's National Register of Historic Places is part of a national program to coordinate and support public and private efforts to identify, evaluate, and protect America's historic and archeological resources.*[33]

The effort to have the shops designated as nationally important involved the creation of a continuance form, a nomination comprehensive enough to catalogue the physical buildings themselves, describe the history and purpose of the site and speak to its example of time in America and American industry. The continuance form notes the shops' importance in several ways. It specifies the period of significance to be 1882–1938. The form states:

> *The Northern Pacific Railroad Shops Historic District is significant in the context of transportation on a state-wide level and on a local level as the*

only remaining complex in Brainerd associated with the Northern Pacific Railroad, the chief employer and economic presence for over one hundred years in Brainerd, Minnesota. This complex is also significant within the architectural and engineering context on a statewide level. It is one of only three relatively intact surviving nineteenth century examples of railroad shops erected for large-scale repair operations.

The structural condition and historic merit of buildings on the site were evaluated and catalogued. Also mentioned were the concrete slabs of the demolished roundhouse. These were described as a "pie shape" as the turntable in the center and the tracks radiating from it now are long gone. Remains of the foundation of the transfer table, though under soil, were noted as apparent.

The continuance form also describes,

Individually and collectively, the buildings remain impressive and largely unaltered representations of nineteenth century industrial architecture and engineering merit. The Brainerd shops are historically significant in the history of the city. Not only does the present city of Brainerd owe its location to the decision of the Northern Pacific Railroad to originally locate its headquarters there, but the railroad shops virtually supported the town and caused its growth and expansion. From approximately 1,400 workers in 1888, the shops still employed 571 workers as late as 1959, a figure which represented an annual payroll of almost 3 million dollars. From the 1870s until the 1960s, the shops at Brainerd were the leading industry in the city.

The nomination was successful. The Northern Pacific Railroad Shops were listed in the National Register of Historic Places as a historic district on January 1, 1989.

Historic designation can give a property status and recognition but is not intended to provide much protection. "Unless the historic site in question receives federal funding, the National Register places no restrictions on what a non-federal owner may do with their property up to and including destruction."[34]

On the state level, there are more protections, especially if state funding is involved. The Minnesota State Historic Preservation Office (SHPO) has a "legal framework and financial incentives," provides technical assistance and environmental review and works with local governments in preservation efforts. It requires review for construction or alterations (mn.gov). The Minnesota Environmental Rights Act (MERA), however, provides broad protection for historic resources, including properties that have not been listed in federal, state or local registers.

REPURPOSE AND REUSE

By the mid-1980s, the effects of the merger of Burlington Northern had resulted in large parts of the railyard becoming vacant. Very important for the survival and historic preservation of buildings on the site, their generally solid physical stability and an active local economy favored their avoidance of demolition.

The large beige brick buildings with their handsome nineteenth-century architecture and skillful engineering design with sizable interior floor areas and lofty ceilinged spaces were very adaptable for new industrial and commercial functions after the railroad discontinued operations.

Potential developers recognized these possibilities. There were enthusiastic visions of what the NP shops site could be in its post-industrial life. Renovation costs would be enormous and would need to be taken in stages.

But as with many industrial locations in the past few centuries, lead, asbestos and other toxic substances resulting from the operations left the surrounding soil contaminated. In fact, the railyard became listed as a Superfund site due to the percentages of lead and other toxic chemicals present. The BNSF (Burlington Northern had merged with the Santa Fe Railroad) remediated the soil to the current regulations of the EPA (Environment Protection Administration), and the matter was considered settled.

In the years to follow, however, changes of ownership and many contentions ensued. To have the NP shops removed from the Superfund listing, cleanup to meet the new more stringent EPA regulations took place. Costs for testing, cleanup and legal suits and countersuits were disputed. What costs could be recovered by the owners through state programs hinged on the definitions of words and intent. It was ruled that nothing would be recovered. Further testing, a Community Involvement Plan and many disputations continued.

The Minnesota Pollution Control Agency partially delisted the shops site in 2015.[35] The site was eventually removed from the Superfund National Priorities List.[36]

While the Brainerd shops are listed in the National Register and have corresponding state recognition, the buildings serve local history even today.

Brainerd would not exist without the Northern Pacific. The shops also serve personal and family histories, having put an indelible stamp on the workers and their family lives. This stamp and these stories are present in the generations of children and grandchildren of shop workers.

The Northern Pacific Center

But it's important that the NP shops also serve the present. Several medium-sized commercial companies subdivided throughout the various buildings had been operating in the railyard even before parts were renovated to make event spaces. More development and renovation occurred in the years since.

Now, it is developed into the Northern Pacific Center, whose website lists several businesses within the complex, including retail shops, a fitness center, a coffee shop and a brewery.[37] More vision and renovation made way for the site's use as a wedding venue. Weddings are promoted as a significant part of its use as an event center. Glamorous photos of the wedding spaces have appeared in bridal magazines as well as on the event center's website.

Large buildings that formerly held workers, tools, machines and their din and grime had once been abandoned. Years later, their walls and windows have undergone interior design treatments. Holiday sales and proms now take place inside some of these spaces. Our cousin Marilyn said, "I have been back to the shops once for an antique sale. They have an event center there and the grounds are used for other events. I saw what was left of a thriving workplace, and I remember fondly my father's working there."

The shop building being prepared for future reuse as an event space. *Minnesota Historical Society.*

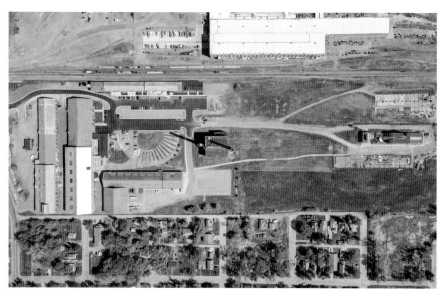

Top: An aerial view of the Northern Pacific Center. *The Northern Pacific Center.*

Bottom: The Shoppes. *Northern Pacific Center.*

Plans to open the mighty power plant have been in the works, a huge project involving clearing out debris and remediating asbestos. According to the website for the Northern Pacific Center, it has been cleared and is prepared for use as a space for weddings and other events. The enormous wheel that had been prominent in the interior will remain.

My daughter Carla imagines Jim Roscoe's laugh at seeing the once noisy, thronging spaces where workers swore and sweated now filled with crystal glasses and pastel tablecloths. That the repurposing has been so drastic makes her laugh, too, but she also remembers her grandpa's deep pragmatism. Successful reuse and financial viability are what was needed.

APPENDIX A
HISTORIC DESIGNATION CONTINUANCE FORM (TEXT)

The nomination for the National Register of Historic Places was approved on January 1, 1989.

The reference number is 88003024. Its National Archives Identifier is 9320157.

The text of the continuance and nomination form is as follows:

The Northern Pacific car repair shops in Brainerd, Minnesota, are located on an east–west axis south of the Northern Pacific railroad tracks on a large rectangular parcel of property. To the north of the property being nominated is a large vacant lot with the new car shops, built in 1945 and still owned by the Burlington Northern Railroad. To the south immediately adjacent to the nominated property is a residential area. East of the site is an undeveloped swampy area, and west is the right-of-way along the tracks. The site is about one-half mile east of downtown Brainerd's central business district.

This nomination consists of ten buildings and two structures (remnants of structures): a transfer table foundation and the foundation of the roundhouse. The shop buildings were constructed with considerable uniformity of style and materials, cream-colored common brick with red wood trim and rusticated sandstone window sills, and date between the years 1882 to 1925. The buildings follow the design established with the first construction in the early 1880s. Subsequent additions, alterations, and new construction were compatible with the first work.

The surviving complex today represents about 15 percent of the complex on both the north and south sides of the tracks as it existed at the end of World War II. Individually, the surviving buildings retain good exterior integrity, with alterations generally limited to window and door alterations (largely through the use of glass block window infill and a few new doors).

Structurally, the buildings are in very good condition and blueprints indicate that the concrete slab foundations were built on pilings to reduce vibrations from the heavy rail traffic near and through the site. However, there are several problems with some details on the buildings. Since the site is low and swampy, the common cream brick in lower courses of most building walls is in deteriorated condition generally with spalling and powdery disintegration due to wicking of water. Most of the buildings need tuckpointing for a foot or two above the ground. All windows and doors are in particularly poor to deteriorated shape. The ten remaining buildings have some 1,500 windows and almost all of them are have [*sic*] rotted frames and are in need of replacement. From 1973 to 1983 when Burlington Northern abandoned the site, the railroad did minimal repairs. The buildings have stood vacant and open to the weather for several years.

The tracks which ran through the site and between the buildings have been removed and the railroad ties have been torn out. At the east end of the site are piles of railroad ties between the buildings. These tracks and the transfer table were torn out between 1981 when operations ceased at the site and 1983 when the Burlington Northern sold the site.

Listed below are the ten buildings and two structures being nominated.

Building 1: Boiler and tank shop (Tank, Cab, and Flue shop, 1882; south extension 1900, 1917). The original building (north portion) was 332 9 "x 80 4 "and one story. It has cream-colored brick walls laid in American bond. The first two bays on the north end of the east facade were sandblasted by a previous owner. The south extension is 238 'x 100 4 "and two stories with a 30 'long monitor. The original building's north portion has a slate roof with missing shingles and the original monitor has been removed. The south extension has a wood gabled monitor with wood-infilled window openings. Roof skylights added after construction in the south extension are not original and the roof is asbestos shingled. Constructed with a stone and concrete block foundation and a steel truss gabled roof, this building has multiple pilastered recessed bays and brick corbelling with wood crown molding under the eaves. Windows are large triple-hung sash with 16/16/16 lights in segmental-arched openings. There are large wood panelled locomotive double doors along the east façade, which was accessed via the transfer table. This building was designed to house a variety of shop operations including paint, cab, flue, and boiler repairs. The building retains almost total exterior integrity.

2. Building 2: Machine Shop (1882; south extension 1900, 1917). The original one story building measured 224′ x 120 8″, the south extension was 331 4½″ x 133 5″ and two stories tall. The construction and design is virtually identical to the boiler and tank shop (Building 1). There is some glass block infill in the window openings and multiple roof skylights. Two small additions on the east (rear) were added in several stages between 1900–1916. The locomotive doors are on the west side facing the transfer table and opposite the locomotive doors on the east side of Building 1. This building was designed to house variety of machining areas including a tin shop, sheet metal shop, and tool shop. With the exception of some of the windows, this building has almost total exterior integrity.

3. Building 3: Blacksmith Shop (1882; east addition 1907, south extension, 1900; alterations, 1924). The design and construction is virtually identical to buildings 1 and 2. The original building is the northern portion and is on an east–west axis. It was one story and 300′ x 80 4″. The 1907 east extension to the original structure was 117′ x 80′ 4″, and the south addition was 126′ x 125 9″. This building was designed to house blacksmith and rail shop operations. With the exception of some recent glass block window infill and the 1962 replacement of the original wood monitor with metal roof turbines, the building retains almost total exterior integrity.

4. Building 4: Warehouse (1923, ca. 1950 east addition). This one story building is approximately 195′ x 38′. It is an uncomplicated cream brick building with a slightly-pitched gabled roof and raised poured concrete foundation with a wood loading platform along the south side covered in corrugated sheet metal. The east addition is concrete block, consists of a 3 stall vehicle garage, and first appears on a 1950 BN plat map. The south side has two newer overhead garage doors. The north side has several wire glass steel windows and two original wood loading dock doors. This building has no decorative elements and, except for the cream brick walls, is not of the quality or style of the other buildings on the site.

5. Building 5: Office and Storehouse Building (1882; eastern extensions built in 1883, 1907, 1918). The earliest section of this building was constructed in 1882 and was increasingly extended to the east. The last eastern addition, built in 1918, has a flat roof, and triple-hung steel awning-type windows setting it apart from the earlier additions. Today, this two story structure is 478′x 436″. The building faces west and is dominated by a pyramidal-roofed clock tower measuring 13′x 13′x 68′. The 1882 portion of the building has two wood gabled roof dormers facing north and south. Constructed of cream-colored Brainerd brick with corbelling and a steel truss-supported hipped roof, it is similar in style and construction to buildings 1 and 2. Walls have multiple pilastered bays on all facades and windows are segmental arched with 6/6, 9/9, and 21/21 double hung sash. Windows are usually paired on the second story and many windows on the south and north facades have been infilled with glass block. The clock is missing from the circular space designed for it. Atop the tower's mansard roof is iron roof cresting and a weathervane in the shape of a railroad engine. A Northern Pacific insignia ("NPRR") is located on the main entrance keystone. This building was designed to contain an extensive supply storage area and office facilities for the shops complex.

6. Building 6: Power Plant (1924–25). This building is three stories with a raised basement. Walls are a yellow-orangy brick and the roof is flat. Recessed pilastered bays are of irregular width with corbelling. Windows are steel framed with wire glass and are in deteriorated condition with much broken and missing glass. The building is flanked east and west by towering concrete chimney stacks and on the north by a wood trestle and coal hopper. Exterior integrity is intact.

7. Building 7: Foundry Boiler House (later Bridge and Building shop), 1910, 1912; east addition, 1917. This building was designed and constructed in a similar manner to buildings 1 and 2. It measures 55′x 50′and has a wood gabled monitor sheathed in corrugated metal. All exterior walls have been sandblasted. The building is L-shaped: the east 1917 addition having been designed to house an air compressor. In 1929, this building was used as a carpenters' shop. Alterations include some red brick or glass brick window infill on the east and north sides, and some newer concrete window sills where rusticated sandstone sills rotted.

8. Building 8: Pattern Shop and Storehouse Building, 1911. This building consists of the pattern shop measuring 804″x 508″x one story and the

pattern storehouse of the same dimensions but four stories tall. The design and construction are similar to buildings 1 and 2. Windows are 16 light steel industrial with wire glass, paired within the pilastered bays. There is a monitor on the low pitched gabled roof. Brick is deteriorated and patched with red and cream-colored brick. There are three newer garage doors on the east one story facade added sometime after 1980. This building was designed to house foundry pattern production and the shop and storage area for the adjacent foundry immediately to the northeast which was razed.

9. Building 9: Acetylene Generator Plant, 1924. This small rectangular building is one story with a slightly-pitched gabled roof, cream brick, and poured concrete foundation. Windows are steel industrial with wire glass. It is similar in style to buildings 1 and 2. It has brick window sills, a soldier course frieze, and plain wood fascia. The brick is deteriorated.

10. Building 10: Lavatory Building, 1907. This one story building is simple in design. It is of cream-colored brick in American bond, with a slightly-pitched gabled roof, segmented arched windows, concrete block foundation, red rusticated sandstone sills and plain wood eaves. It sits west of Building 1.

11. Structure 11: Roundhouse foundation, 1882 with subsequent extension on the east side to accommodate larger engines. What remains of this building, razed in 1960, is the concrete slabs in pie shape between what were the tracks. The center turntable is gone as are all the tracks. The building was cream brick and a few of the lower wall bricks are loose and on the ground. The original building had been altered and repaired extensively in 1907.

12. Structure 12: Transfer table foundation, 1882, 1901, 1906, 1907, 1915. The electric transfer table was located between buildings 1 and 2 and was mounted on four rails in the transfer pit. The table itself measured 38' and consisted of a single track table, cab, and an electrical mount to the overhead catenary cables. It was designed to transfer locomotives and cars from the spur line at the north end of buildings 1 and 2 south and into the locomotive pits in the interiors. The north quarter of the pit was removed before 1980 and the remainder was removed around 1981. Soil has been brought in between the two buildings, but it is apparent that some of the concrete foundation of the transfer table still remains.

The Northern Pacific Railroad Shops Historic District is significant in the context of transportation on a state-wide level and on a local level as the only remaining complex in Brainerd associated with the Northern Pacific Railroad, the chief employer and economic presence for over one hundred years in Brainerd, Minnesota. This complex is also significant within the context of architecture and engineering on a statewide level. It is one of only three relatively intact surviving nineteenth century examples of railroad shops erected for large-scale repair operations. The other two, the Jackson Street shops of the Saint Paul, Minneapolis, and Manitoba Railway Company, and the Como Avenue shops of the Northern Pacific Railway Company, both located in Saint Paul, are already listed on the National Register. Although the Brainerd shops were the first and largest Northern Pacific repair complex, today the oldest remaining buildings there date from 1882 and are contemporary with the buildings at the Jackson Street shops. The Como shop site, also on the National Register, opened in 1885 when it took over certain functions initially done for the Northern Pacific at the Brainerd shops. At the end of [the] first full year after the original buildings in this nomination were constructed, the complex was hailed as "the most extensive shops to be found on the Northern Pacific Road," according to Eugene V. Smalley's 1883 *History of the Northern Pacific Railroad*. The buildings and structures in this nomination are significant for the period 1882–1938.

The city of Brainerd owed its existence to the Northern Pacific railroad. The railroad's decision in 1870 to locate the crossing of the Mississippi River at the present site of Brainerd spelled the death of Crow Wing, the earlier settlement to the south. For this reason, Brainerd was first known as "The Crossing." The railroad chose Brainerd as its headquarters in 1871, locating there its Second Empire style General Headquarters building, the car shops, and the railroad hospital. The car repair shops were the most extensive on the line and ranked among the best in the nation in 1888.

The first shop buildings, built in the early 1870s, were on the north side of the tracks across from the present parcel and were all wood frame. They burned in 1886 in a huge fire. These first structures were supplemented by Buildings 1, 2, 3, and 5 on the south side of the tracks in 1882. Initial operations at the site were devoted to repairs to steam locomotives and manufacture of various parts for wood- and later coal-burning steam locomotives for distribution to other repair shops along the line of the Northern Pacific system. In the late 1880s, the Brainerd shops employed 722 men in the locomotive department and 344 in the car department. Brainerd was the headquarters for the engineer's department for the entire road and the headquarters of the operating department of all the main line and branches of the Northern Pacific in Minnesota. Three divisions of the road terminated at Brainerd.

In 1882, the Northern Pacific began surveying land to establish a line between Minneapolis and Saint Paul and, in 1883, bought the site for the Como repair shops, which were opened in 1886. Passenger car maintenance and erection was then transfered [*sic*] from the Brainerd shops to the newly opened Como shops.

The Brainerd shops were the oldest major locomotive repair facility on the Northern Pacific line. At its facilities, locomotives could be completely rebuilt, and in one case, an entire locomotive was built at Brainerd. Until the early 20th century, most of the major rebuilding of locomotives was done there. The Northern Pacific classified steam locomotive repair into five categories from Class 1 extensive repairs involving replacement parts and new boilers to Class 5 light repairs, such as refitting or replacing brasses and repairing machinery. The Brainerd shops were set up to do any class of repairs. But each division point on the line also had roundhouses for locomotive repairs and maintenance and small engine houses were located in smaller towns for emergency repairs. Between 1925 and 1945, there were three major locomotive shops operated by the Northern Pacific: Brainerd; South Tacoma, Washington; and Livingston, Montana. Next oldest after Branierd [*sic*] were the repair shops in South Tacoma. They did all classes of repairs for locomotives at the extreme western end of the line. After World War I, the South Tacoma shops took on added work and the facilities were expanded accordingly. Until the 1920s, the locomotive repair shops at Livingston, Montana, were only a divisional shop comparable to those at Missoula, Pasco and Duluth. Beginning in the 1920s and after the divisions were restructured in 1932, the Livingston shops took on added importance because of their location midway between Brainerd and South Tacoma. Because they represented the newest facility for locomotive repairs, work was increasingly transfered [*sic*] to Livingston after 1945.

Through the early 20th century, the Branierd [*sic*] shops handled such locomotive repairs as replacing fire boxes and flues. This was done in the Boiler shop (Building 3). The reaching shop in Building 2 repaired such things as flues, caps, hollow bolts, throat sheets, ash pans, and front end appliances and installed new cyclones. The Parker Topping Foundry Company building on the shops site supplied castings for the entire railroad system east of Spokane, Washington, and employed 150 men in 1890. The Saint Paul Foundry was also used as a supplier for needed castings.

The foundry building on the Branierd [*sic*] site was closed after the 1922 national rail workers' strike and a new foundry was built off-site. During its operating years, however, it manufactured brass, bronze, aluminum and grey iron castings for new parts and accessories. In addition to repairing locomotives, the Brainerd shops also repaired and rebuilt ore cars for use in northern Minnesota mines and the Northern Pacific owned coal mines in the Rosebud region of Montana.

After World War II, the function of the shops shifted from construction and repair of cars and locomotives to service as a reclamation facility, a function it served for the entire Burlington Northern system until the facility was closed in 1981. Locomotive repairs were largely moved to Livingston, Montana, around 1951. By 1964, the Boiler, Pipe, and Tin shop (building 1) was devoted to manufacture and repairs of tank work, bridge and ore dock, earth moving, right-of-way equipment, and other phases of steel, sheet metal, and pipe work. The Machine Shop and Tool Room (building 2) was used to repair and manufacture cranes, pile drivers, wreckers, earth moving machines, machines used for track work, switch parts, equipment for drilling and machining of various metals, and repair of diesel axles and freight car wheels. At the same time, the Blacksmith shop (building 3) was repairing and manufacturing numerous items used on the entire railroad, such as track and tool work (switches, frogs, cross-overs, and related track parts and equipment). The Blacksmith shop also was manufacturing forgings for new railroad cars constructed in the 1945 new car shops on the north side of the tracks. The Northern Pacific and the Great Northern merged in 1970 and the Brainerd shops became the property of the Burlington Northern. Burlington Northern sold the site in 1983 and the shops stood vacant until the current developer purchased the site in 1988.

The Brainerd repair shop buildings are significant in the area of architecture and engineering. As a complex, they were maintained with amazing architectural uniformity and consistency. The brick for the 1880s buildings is a common cream brick manufactured locally by William Schwartz brickyard, in business between 1880–1888. The Northern Pacific had its own architects and these buildings were designed to be compatible and are, in fact, very similar to the buildings erected in 1885 at the Como shops in Saint Paul. Individually and collectively, the buildings remain impressive and largely unaltered representations of nineteenth century industrial architecture and engineering skills. Roofs are trussed and were originally either slate or metal. Some of the slate remains. Window sills are rusticated sandstone and all the older buildings have brick corbelling and pilastered bays. These buildings represent a remarkably intact surviving complex of nineteenth century railroad shops erected for large scale operations. Most of the significant large shop buildings have survived changes in function without demolition or extensive exterior alteration. The exceptions on the south side of the tracks are the roundhouse, built in 1882 and subsequently expanded, which sat south of building 5 and the Parker Topping Foundry Company building which was located north of building 8. The roundhouse was razed in 1960 and the foundry at an unknown date after 1923 and before 1969. The remainder of the razed buildings on the site consisted of small buildings such as a sheet iron house, toilets, oil houses, the auto air brake shop, a forging storage house, tool house, blacksmith shop fan room, cooling tower, etc. These buildings were all small, clustered around the extant structures, and generally not measuring over 10 x 15 feet. Burlington Northern Railroad tore most of these down in 1969, according to a plat map.

The Brainerd shops are historically significant in the history of the city. Not only does the present city of Brainerd owe its location to the decision of the Northern Pacific Railroad to locate its headquarters there, but the railroad shops virtually supported the town and caused its growth and expansion. From a high of around 1,400 workers in 1888, the shops still employed 571 workers as late as 1959, a figure which represented an annual payroll of almost 3 million dollars. From the 1870s until the 1960s, the shops at Brainerd were the leading industry in the city. In the 1920s, a history of the city claimed that at least ninety percent of the families were dependent on the shops. The city still sports many small mechanics cottages which were built for the highly skilled machine and engine workers. Historically, the shops and the city suffered a severe blow during the 1922 national rail workers' strike. Many men lost their jobs when they honored union picket lines and became permanently unemployed. Scabs were brought in and created much tension and violence in the city. From 1925 on, the shops gradually did less and less repair work and the city tried to distance itself, not very successfully, from the events at the shops. Nonetheless, the shops remained a vital and important economic force until closed in 1981.

COMPREHENSIVE FEATURE ARTICLE IN THE *BRAINERD DISPATCH*

The October 9, 1978 issue of the *Brainerd Dispatch* reported:

END OF AN ERA—Bob McGinnis, material manager for Burlington Northern Railroad, takes a last look at buildings scheduled for demolition this year at the Brainerd shops as part of a $1.7 million improvement project. Among the structures slated for the wrecking ball is the main office—better known as the "Tower"—a part of Brainerd's railroad history since 1881.

The Burlington Northern Railroad shops, those massive stone and brick buildings that date back more than 100 years, have a date with the wrecking ball.

The announcement listed eight of the 12 buildings at the shops—everything south of the railroad tracks—will be leveled this year in a $1.7 million modernization move. The historic buildings, seven of which date to 1881 and one to 1871 have become costly white elephants, said Bob McGinnis material manager at the shops.

"They've out-lived their usefulness," he said.

History is one thing, McGinnis said. Economic survival is another.

"They say we've got to save these majestic old buildings," he said. "Well, who is going to pay to maintain them?"

Here at that time is what was intended be demolished:

    —The main south store building, better known as the "Tower 7," built in 1871.

    —The boiler shop.

    —The machine shop.

    —The former blacksmith shop.

—The pattern shop.
—The bridge and building department headquarters.
—The power plant.
—The former paint and sign shop.

Here is what will stay:
—The storage shed for the Bridge and Building Department.
—The main car shop. Bridge and Building will be relocated to this structure.
—The main car store, with the system's electricians housed here.
—The surplus shed.

The downtown depot, which will house communication, linemen and signal maintainers, will also be kept, McGinnis said. "This whole side of the property will be vacated," he said, his arm sweeping the area south of the tracks. "We're putting the entire south side into the north side."

McGinnis conducted a tour of the shops, to show what he meant when he said that "things are bad" with the shops' buildings.

In the old boiler shop, $300,000 has been appropriated for roof repair. "People are getting afraid to go up on the roof on this thing," McGinnis said.

In the power plant, coal boilers provide the shops with steam heat and compressed air for pneumatic tools.

"Steam heat involves water treatment, maintenance, return lines," McGinnis said. He pointed to some nearby tracks, where steam hissed from the ground.

"When you've got a steam leak out between the tracks somewhere and it's 40 below it's a miserable job," he said. "There's a tremendous expense in a system like this."

Lighting in most of the buildings is inadequate, McGinnis said. The water filtration system is obsolete. The engineering department has people going back and forth from one building to another.

The modernization will update the air brake department and make the engineering department more cost-efficient. Different departments will no longer have separate machines, but instead each machine will be "community property," used by both departments.

The coal-fired power plant will be replaced by boilers using diesel fuel and natural gas, with offices heated electrically. Foremen's offices will be relocated to the departments which they oversee, and materials will be housed closer to the work site.

"My maintenance for this facility," McGinnis said, "is going to be cut right down."

A native of Saint Paul, McGinnis started with Northern Pacific in 1944, and moved to Brainerd from Chicago in 1977. He has seen the times when Burlington Northern had more cars in storage than other systems owned and, now, the rumors that the shops might disappear entirely from Brainerd. "Right now, the thing that is confronting all of us is the economy," he said. Also, large power and grain companies now own their own cars, instead of using railroad-owned cars.

"If I were in that business, I would be doing the same thing," McGinnis said. "But it hurts the railroad because we've lost a lot of repair business."

The shops at one time employed 1,200 people, with an annual payroll of $2.9 million. The current head count at the shops is about 180, McGinnis said.

He didn't say so, but a streamlining of the operation at the shops obviously means fewer people. McGinnis made no predictions on numbers, but said that, "Whatever is going to happen should happen this year."

McGinnis continued:

"We anticipate that our manpower situation will be stabilized by the first of the year," he said.

Despite the drop in railroad employment here, the shops still remain a potent force in community buying power, McGinnis said, with a $500,000 annual payroll.

"Yes, there's less people employed here, but we must be number four in terms of payroll," he said. Burlington Northern has instituted packet purchasing, buying supplies locally if possible. McGinnis estimates that the material department spends $4,500 locally per month, while the tie plant spends $1,000 a month.

The shops' refuse bill, landfill charges and utilities total about $16,000 a month, he said.

"These are some dollars being pumped into the community by the BN system," he said.

When he moved to Brainerd, McGinnis said, one of the first questions he was asked was why the railroad moved him here from Chicago when the shops were going to eventually close anyway.

Plans to modernize the shops, he said, should help squelch those rumors.

"The positive thing about all this is that, if BN is spending $1.7 million here, they're obviously not going to shut us down next week. The railroad is not going to disappear. It would be senseless to spend this kind of money on our facility if you were in fact going to shut it down."

What eventually occurred:

In 1982, six Burlington Northern Railroad massive masonry buildings dating back more than 100 years, fell to the wrecking ball, as well as miscellaneous small buildings, one to 1871, became…economically infeasible structures in terms of current railroad operations at that time.

What buildings were demolished:

—The boiler shop.

—The machine shop.

—The former blacksmith shop.

—The pattern shop.

—The Bridge and Building Department headquarters.

—The former paint and sign shop.

What buildings remained:

—The main south administrative and store building, better known as the "Tower" built in 1871.

—The storage shed for the Bridge and Building Department.

—The main Car Shop. Bridge and Building was relocated to this structure.

—The main car store, with the system's electricians housed here.

—The surplus shed.

—The downtown depot, which would house communication, linemen and signal maintainers, was retained

Although the railroad buildings were listed on the National Register of Historic Places, the listing is considered to be honorific, and has no protection from demolition unless federal funds are involved, which was not the case here.

NOTES

1. Carl A. Zapffe, *Oldtimers: Stories of Our Pioneers in the Cass and Crow Wing Lake Region*, vol. 2 (Minneapolis: Colwell Press, 1946).
2. Ann M. Nelson, "The Northern Pacific Rail Road in Brainerd," accessed February 2, 2020, crowwinghistory.org.
3. The Ojibwe People's Dictionary, Department of American Indian Studies, University of Minnesota, accessed July 20, 2022, ojibwe.lib.umn.edu.
4. Jeremy S. Jackson. "Brainerd's Naming Origins Might Not Be the Story Everyone's Heard Before," *Brainerd Dispatch*, August 23, 2020.
5. Zappfe, *Oldtimers II*.
6. Nelson, "Northern Pacific."
7. Ibid.
8. *Brainerd Dispatch*, December 16, 1887.
9. James B. Hedges, *The Colonization Work of the Northern Pacific Railroad*, 1926, MNHS collections.
10. Ann M. Nelson, "A Brief History of Early Northeast Brainerd," accessed June 14, 2022, crowwinghistory.org.
11. *Brainerd Dispatch*, Centennial Edition, 1871–1971.
12. Nelson, "Northeast Brainerd."
13. *Brainerd Tribune*, December 24, 1881.
14. Nelson, "Northern Pacific."
15. Adam Burns, "Railroad Turntables," accessed September 2022, american-rails.com.
16. *Minneapolis Tribune*, March 29, 1886.

17. *Minneapolis Tribune*, March 30, 1886.

18. *Brainerd Dispatch*, Centennial Edition, 1871–1971.

19. *Brainerd Dispatch*, July 14, 1893.

20. Nelson, "Northern Pacific."

21. Ibid.

22. Ibid.

23. "Brick Structure of the Month," accessed June 2022, mnbricks.com.

24. Zappfe, *Oldtimers*.

25. The Living New Deal, "New Deal Timeline," accessed September 5, 2022, https://livingnewdeal.org/what-was-the-new-deal/timeline/.

26. Ibid.

27. Frank Lee, "Bataan Death March Hits Home for Brainerd Families," *Brainerd Dispatch*, April 4, 2022.

28. Adam Burns, "Northern Pacific Railway, *Main Street of the Northwest,*" *accessed September 2022*, https://www.american-rails.com/np.html.

29. *Brainerd Dispatch*, Centennial Edition, 1871–1971.

30. *Brainerd Dispatch*, Centennial Edition, 1871–1971.

31. Steve Raetz, "What Is a Railroad Boxcar & Why Are Their Numbers Declining?," accessed July 6, 2015, https://www.chrobinson.com/it-it/resources/blog/what-does-decreasing-boxcar-fleet-mean-for-u-s-capacity.

32. Adam Burns, "Boxcars: From The 1830's to Contemporary Times," revised April 6, 2022, originally accessed June 12, 2021, https://www.american-rails.com/box.html.

33. National Park Service, "National Register of Historic Places," originally accessed October 2022, https://www.nps.gov/subjects/nationalregister/index.htm.

34. Ibid.

35. Minnesota Pollution Control Agency, "Minnesota Groundwater Contamination Atlas," originally accessed October 2022, https://webapp.pca.state.mn.us/cleanup/search?id=188332-AREA000000000.

36. United States Environmental Protection Agency, "Superfund Site Information: Burlington Northern Brainerd Car Shops," originally accessed October 2022, https://cumulis.epa.gov/supercpad/CurSites/csitinfo.cfm?id=0503691.

37. Northern Pacific Center official website, originally accessed October 2022, northernpacificcenter.com.

BIBLIOGRAPHY

Brainerd Dispatch. "The Brainerd Shops Buildings Face the Wrecking Ball."
    October 9, 1978
———. Centennial Edition, 1871–1971
———. "Re: the Power Plant." December 30, 1920.
"Brick Structure of the Month." Accessed June 2022. mnbricks.com.
Burns, Adam. "Boxcars: From The 1830's To Contemporary Times." Revised
    April 6, 2022. Originally accessed June 12, 2021. american-rails.com.
———. "Northern Pacific Railway, *Main Street of the Northwest.*" Accessed
    September 2022. american-rails.com.
———. "Railroad Turntables." Accessed August 2022. american-rails.com.
Crow Wing County Historical Society website. crowwinghistory.org.
Dillan, Ingolf. *Brainerd's Half Century.* Minneapolis: General Printing
    Company, 1923.
Hedges, James B. *The Colonization Work of the Northern Pacific Railroad.* 1926,
    MNHS collections.
Jackson, Jeremy S. "Brainerd's Naming Origins Might Not Be the Story
    Everyone's Heard Before." *Brainerd Dispatch*, August 23, 2020.
Lee, Frank. "Bataan Death March Hits Home for Brainerd Families."
    Brainerd Dispatch, April 4, 2022.
The Living New Deal. "New Deal Timeline." Accessed September 5,
    2022. https://livingnewdeal.org/what-was-the-new-deal/timeline.
Minneapolis Tribune. Article headed by Northern Pacific. March 29, 1886.

Minnesota Pollution Control Agency. "Minnesota Groundwater Contamination Atlas." Originally accessed October 2022. https://webapp.pca.state.mn.us/cleanup/search/superfund?text=BURLINGTON%20NORTHERN%20CAR%20SHOPS%20(Brainerd)&siteId=188332-AREA0000000001.

Minnesota Public Radio. *Friday Morning Marketplace Report*, September 5, 2014.

National Archives Catalog. "Minnesota SP Northern Pacific Railroad Shops Historic District." Originally accessed via the National Register of Historic Places section of the National Park Service website on numerous occasions in the last few decades. https://catalog.archives.gov/id/93201576.

Nelson, Ann M. "A Brief History of Early Northeast Brainerd." June 18, 2016. crowwinghistory.org.

———. "Northern Pacific Rail Road in Brainerd." February 16, 2019. crowwinghistory.org.

Northern Pacific Center. "Current Information for the Northern Pacific Center." Accessed October 2022. northernpacificcenter.com.

Ojibwe People's Dictionary. Department of American Indian Studies, University of Minnesota. Accessed July 20, 2022. ojibwe.lib.umn.edu.

Peterson, Harold F. "Early Minnesota Railroads and the Quest for Settlers." *Minnesota Historical Society Magazine*, March 1932, 25–44. collections.mnhs.org/MNHistoryMagazine/articles/13/v13i01p025-044.pdf.

Raetz, Steve. "What Is a Railroad Boxcar & Why Are Their Numbers Declining?" October 6, 2015. https://www.chrobinson.com/it-it/resources/blog/what-does-decreasing-boxcar-fleet-mean-for-u-s-capacity.

United States Environmental Protection Agency. "Superfund Site Information: Burlington Northern Brainerd Car Shops." Originally accessed October 2022. https://cumulis.epa.gov/supercpad/CurSites/csitinfo.cfm?id=0503691.

Zappfe, Carl A. *Oldtimers: Stories of Our Pioneers in the Cass and Crow Wing Lake Region*. Vol. 2. Minneapolis: Colwell Press, 1946.

ABOUT THE AUTHOR

Bob Roscoe has been an architect and historic preservationist for over fifty years. He studied art history and architecture at the University of Minnesota. He was a partner in the architectural firm Roark Kramer Roscoe Design for fifteen years and served for twenty-one years on the Minneapolis Heritage Preservation Commission. He has been involved with several historic preservation groups, including Preserve Minneapolis.

In the early 1970s, he was part of the project area committee that worked to save Milwaukee Avenue's rows of houses originally built for Milwaukee railroad workers, which became designated as a historic district with his involvement. He drafted architectural plans for houses being rehabilitated and designed the pedestrian mall that replaced the street.

For eight years, he served as editor of the *Minnesota Preservationist*, published by the Preservation Alliance of Minnesota, and wrote a column called "Endangered" that was published in *Architecture Minnesota Magazine* by AIA Minnesota.

In 2014, he authored the book *Milwaukee Avenue: Community Renewal in Minneapolis*, also published by The History Press. With his brother John Roscoe, he was coauthor of the book *Legacies of Faith: The Catholic Churches of Stearns County, Minnesota*, published in 2009 by North Star Press of St. Cloud. He is currently working on a book entitled "Rice Park, St. Paul: An Intimate Enclosure Brings Grace to a City."

He and his wife, Sally, have two children, Carla and Neal, and care for two reasonably trouble-free dogs.

He is very much the proud son of a shop dog.

Visit us at
www.historypress.com